THE Secrets OF EXCEPTIONAL COUNSELORS

Jeffrey A. Kottler

American Counseling Association
6101 Stevenson Avenue, Suite 600
Alexandria, VA 22304
www.counseling.org

American Counseling Association
6101 Stevenson Avenue, Suite 600
Alexandria, VA 22304

Associate Publisher Carolyn C. Baker

Digital and Print Development Editor Nancy Driver

Senior Production Manager Bonny E. Gaston

Production Coordinator Karen Thompson

Copy Editor Beth Ciha

Cover and text design by Bonny E. Gaston

Libarary of Congress Cataloging-in-Publication Data
Names: Kottler, Jeffrey A., author.
Title: The secrets of exceptional counselors / Jeffrey A. Kottler.
Description: Alexandria, VA : American Counseling Association, [2017] | Includes bibliographical references and index.
Identifiers: LCCN 2017015993 | ISBN 9781556203787 (pbk.: alk. paper)
Subjects: LCSH: Counselors. | Counseling.
Classification: LCC BF636.6 .K6855 2017 | DDC 158.3—dc23 LC record available at https://lccn.loc.gov/2017015993

This book is dedicated to Jon Carlson
My coauthor, colleague, friend, and brother
1945–2017

• • •

Table of Contents

Preface: Tricks of the Trade

Every profession has certain secrets of the guild. Passed on from one generation to the next throughout the ages, these are the lessons taught from wide experience. They are sometimes shortcuts that save time, or else ways to operate more efficiently and effectively while minimizing resources and reducing effort. Sometimes they include ways that maximize profits or even shortchange clients or customers through deceptive practices. Sales staff in car dealerships, for instance, are known to rely on particular methods to manipulate customers into purchasing options they don't really need, telling men that automatic door locks are for convenience while telling women that they are for safety. Waitresses in certain restaurants are required to dress seductively in tight-fitting, low-cut dresses. They are taught to lean forward when taking an order from a man to maximize the display, whereas they are inclined to kneel by the table to deemphasize this feature with other women. Mountain climbers have their little tricks as well, passed along from guides, to make their lives in treacherous environments a little more comfortable, such as using duct tape to prevent blisters or hanging their wet socks with dental floss. Magicians have their secret methods of redirection, sleight of hand, and illusions, all intended to capitalize on disguised or hidden actions beyond public view.

We counselors have our professional secrets as well to improve our functioning, most of which I hope are designed to better serve our clients. But some exceptions also rely on duplicity in order to increase our power and influence. We pretend to know more than we do, stall for time when we are stumped, and occasionally enhance our standing by appearing like magicians. However, we are also highly skilled in communication and relational engagement and thus able to read audiences accurately to know when things are working and when they are not.

One counselor I know was quite proud of the ways he had discovered to appear far more masterful than he actually felt most of the time. He loved to operate from a position of unquestioned authority and dominance, much like the Wizard of Oz. His clients were quite impressed, even astounded at times, by his seemingly mystical powers to read minds, predict the future, and even mysteriously always know exactly when the session was over even though he never wore a watch and had no direct access to a clock. In fact, the only timepiece in the room was a single small device that was actually situated next to him out of his direct view. It was a frequent topic of conversation that his clients brought up: How did he always know when time was up? He would just shrug.

This counselor, for reasons that went beyond client welfare, enjoyed using certain secrets and tricks to fool his clients into believing that he had powers that went way beyond those of mortal beings. It turns out that he had meticulously arranged his office in such a way that he could appear to be looking directly at his client while seeing the image of the clock next to him reflected in the glass of a picture hanging on the wall. He was so devious in this regard that it wasn't even a direct reflection, which might be too easy for the client to figure out; instead, the reflection of the clock bounced off the glass of one framed picture to actually become visible in another one on a side wall. So he could appear to be thoughtfully considering some idea while staring at a side wall and then suddenly announce that time was up. The client would then look around the room and wonder how the heck this counselor always knew the exact time, as if he had a clock inside his head. Of course nowadays smartwatches can aid counselors with hidden signals to accomplish the same goal of enhancing illusions of power.

I mention this example as the sort of secret within our profession that I do *not* wish to investigate—one that involves deception or manipulation, even if supposedly designed to improve effectiveness. Instead, I am interested in those ideas, behaviors, strategies, methods, interventions, and even little tricks learned over time that exceptional counselors have invented, inherited, developed, borrowed, stolen, or discovered that increase both professional effectiveness and personal satisfaction. I have attempted to collect and catalogue the greatest wisdom of some of the best clinicians, especially those among us who have worked long and hard to find ways to increase their effectiveness and efficiency through innovation, creativity, and dogged determination to better serve their clients.

I have been especially curious about some of the things that experienced counselors have learned, or devised for themselves and their work, that have previously gone unmentioned—or at least rarely acknowledged in a meaningful way. There has been some limited research in this area by investigators such as Barry Duncan and Scott Miller describing the way that exemplary clinicians or "supershrinks" have developed certain signature habits, such as continually asking their clients how they're doing and making adjustments accordingly, as well as simply devoting themselves wholeheartedly to achieving excellence in their work.

Throughout the past few decades I have been privileged, along with my partner Jon Carlson, to interview some of the most prominent and influential theoreticians and practitioners in our field. We were able to talk to them about some of their most unusual cases, creative breakthroughs, spiritual transcendence, greatest successes, advocacy efforts, disappointing failures, and disturbing deceptions; the clients who changed them the most; as well as their own developmental adjustments over time. During these conversations, these seminal thinkers, researchers, and clinicians revealed some of their secrets that had rarely been mentioned previously. Many disclosed, for example, that they no longer practiced the models associated with their names, having moved beyond single-theory allegiance to a far more pragmatic, integrative, flexible approach. Others mentioned the personal journeys that had led them to settle on a particular brand of helping that reflected their unique personalities, values, and preferences. There were even a few who shared their own doubts and uncertainties about the extent to which their contributions really mattered.

Although my previous focus was to target specific kinds of lessons that had been learned by eminent counselors and therapists—for instance, how they recovered from disappointments or which clients were most memorable or challenging—I am now interested in expanding this lens to encompass a far broader view of knowledge and wisdom that may have been long buried or ignored. For beginners and veterans alike, I am pleased to reveal some of the secrets and tricks of the trade that ordinarily receive little attention.

As we are all quite aware, there are so many different theories and hypotheses regarding what makes a truly excellent therapist. There are trait theories that look at personality features. There are particular training models that are purported to deliver optimal results. Advanced degrees, postgraduate workshops, supervision—are all alleged to play a role. But ultimately, beyond a requisite level of intelligence and emotional functioning, the best among us are quite simply those who have worked hardest to develop themselves. They are intensely motivated and committed to becoming the best practitioners of their craft—and they are willing to make all kinds of personal sacrifices and devote time and energy in order to make that a reality.

It's not just the so-called 10,000-hour rule, popularized by Malcolm Gladwell, that implies consistent, dedicated, reflective practice over time; it is also a matter of caring deeply about being the absolute best at what they do. Exceptional counselors have a secret that really isn't much of a secret at all: They just flat out work harder than the rest of us. I mean this not so much in terms of the number of hours they devote to their craft, how long they've been in practice, or what kind of degrees and credentials they've accumulated but rather in terms of their sheer grit and determination. They rarely feel discouraged and tend to dig in harder when they face challenges or disappointments.

I am talking about passion and excitement for the work, for the people they are helping, the kind that doesn't diminish over time. It has sometimes been noted that longtime veterans in our field can become complacent over time, slip into familiar routines, treat the calling as just a job. They think they've seen it all before. They start just going through the motions, following a long-established pattern that gets the job done, all without much drama or even concerted effort.

What about those among us who are truly exceptional? Such professionals adopt an unwavering attitude of passion for what they do. They are constantly reinventing themselves. They test their limits. They push themselves to discover new ways of operating, perhaps rendering what they'd already been doing obsolete. Rather than resenting or resisting such continuous upgrades and growth, they welcome such opportunities as the primary means by which to remain fresh and completely engaged.

Acknowledgments

My lifelong friend, colleague, coauthor, and brother, Jon Carlson was my partner in the original conception of this book. We had a number of conversations about the nature of this project, and he was instrumental in identifying many of the professionals whose voices you will hear throughout these pages. Unfortunately, he never lived long enough to actually begin writing. As I write these words, I am still mourning the loss of one of my oldest friends. Jon and I had completed a dozen books together, and this one was to be our seminal work, collecting the most cherished secrets of friends and colleagues as well as sharing some of our own best practices that we have held close to our vests throughout our 45-year careers. Jon isn't around to see how this book eventually came together, but even during his last weeks, sitting by the window in his Wisconsin home in the woods, watching the birds, we shared back and forth what we hoped this book could become. Jon died just a few weeks later.

I am grateful to the following counselors and therapists who shared their secrets: Lori Ash, Leah Brew, Jose Cervantes, Thelma Duffey, Barry Duncan, Liz Eddy, Miguel Gallardo, Carrie Grubisic, Michael Hoyt, Amanda Johnson, Philip Kirk, Stephen Lankton, Mayra Martinez, John Murphy, Ryan Neace, Sarah Pemberton, Kimberlin Phillips, Daya Singh Sandhu, Jackie Scherer, Mary Schor, Chris Williams, and Michael Yapko.

I'm also grateful to Carolyn Baker, Nancy Driver, and the staff at the American Counseling Association for their support and assistance in the development of this project.

About the Author

Jeffrey A. Kottler, PhD, is one of the most prominent authors in the fields of counseling, psychotherapy, health, and education, having written more than 90 books on a wide range of subjects. Some of his most highly regarded works include *On Being a Therapist; Introduction to Counseling: Voices From the Field; Learning Group Leadership; Creative Breakthroughs in Therapy; Bad Therapy; The Client Who Changed Me; Stories We've Heard, Stories We've Told: Life-Changing Narratives in Therapy and Everyday Life; The Therapist in the Real World; On Being a Master Therapist; Relationships in Counseling and the Counselor's Life;* and *Therapy Over 50.*

Jeffrey has been a counselor, supervisor, and educator for 45 years, working in preschool, middle school, mental health center, crisis center, hospital, nongovernmental organization, university, community college, private practice, and disaster relief settings. He served as a Fulbright scholar and senior lecturer in Peru and Iceland as well as worked as a visiting professor in New Zealand, Australia, Hong Kong, Singapore, and Nepal. Jeffrey is professor emeritus of counseling at California State University, Fullerton. He currently lives in Houston, where he works on projects related to refugee trauma and is clinical professor of psychiatry at Baylor College of Medicine.

CHAPTER 1

A Tough Lesson That Forever Changed the Way I Work

I was waiting anxiously in my office, listening for the sound of the door opening in the waiting room to signal the arrival of my new client. I had just launched my private practice a few months earlier, and I was struggling to meet even basic expenses. It was a misguided and naïve belief that I could just hang out my shingle, so to speak, and expect that people would come flocking to my door or that referral sources would deliver as promised. In fact, I had a grand total of four clients in my caseload. Oh yeah, plus this new referral, which would boost my practice by 20%!

I briefly mentioned this story in a previous book with Rick Balkin about the importance of relationships in counseling, but it bears describing in further depth to emphasize one of the secrets of exceptional counselors: their ability to connect immediately with a new client during an initial consultation. After all, the overriding goal of any initial interview is *not* just to collect information, as well as to form a diagnosis and treatment plan, but rather to get the client to return for a *second* appointment! If we can't secure that commitment, nothing else really matters, no matter how comprehensive the data we collected.

I had scheduled my precious few clients throughout the week, which means that I would go into the office to fool around, make calls, try to pretend like I had a full-time job, and then wait for my single appointment. This was a Friday, the one day of the week that I had promised never to book, but it was the only time my new client said was convenient. I was so desperate for business that I decided not to negotiate.

I arrived at my office a few hours earlier than the single scheduled appointment, supposedly to do paperwork but really just to create the illusion I had something to do. I would stare out the window across the street at a retail strip of establishments selling obscure products. One in particular that caught my eye was a place called Flute World. I wondered how one could possibly earn a living selling a single kind of musical instrument, especially one that wasn't exactly very popular. With time to spare, I actually decided to walk across the street and check the place out, then impulsively bought a flute to play with as a means of occupying myself during frequent idle times waiting for the world to discover me.

Once I assembled the instrument, with no real clue how to produce actual music, I realized that it might be a good idea to schedule some lessons, perhaps even begin after my new client left this afternoon. After all, I had little else to do. I actually started calculating in my head how much flute instruction I might be able to afford after I collected my fee.

"Self-discipline and prudence!" I reminded myself. After all, I had expenses to cover and a family to support.

I reviewed my notes regarding the person who would soon be arriving. She had been referred by her physician, whose office was in the building. I could feel my excitement building: If things worked out well and I did a good job, maybe the good doctor would send a stream of future patients and I'd be well on my way. But for now, all I knew was that she was presenting symptoms of extreme anxiety and there didn't appear to be any organic cause. "Let me know what you think," the internist instructed me. "I'm just at a loss other than to up her prescription of Xanax."

Already I had reviewed my books and resources about all the nuances, symptoms, causes, and precipitating factors associated with anxiety. Next I had consulted the *Physicians' Desk Reference* to study the dosages, side effects, and contraindications related to her medication. In other words, I had invested a tremendous amount of time and energy into preparing myself to function at my absolute best.

I put the flute away. Then I sat at my desk, drumming my fingers, willing time to speed up. If the clock sometimes seems to move glacially slow when you are sitting in a session that seems to be going nowhere, it is positively maddening when you are waiting for a new client. I always feel nervous in such circumstances, wondering whether I will know what to do or even whether I've lost my healing magic. During those first few minutes after meeting a new client I often feel a surge of panic once the person begins to speak. I usually feel lost and confused, stumbling around trying to get a handle on what might be going on and what I should do about it. I am often filled with doubts regarding whether I even have anything meaningful to offer. I start to question the legitimacy of what I'm doing: Is it really enough just to *talk* about problems? Will these sessions actually put in a dent in the chronic suffering that has so far been impervious to any other action or intervention?

I studied for the sixth or seventh time the brief notes that I had scribbled down after my initial phone call with the expected client: *Unmarried. Early 30s. Possible anxiety disorder. Doctor says she's skittish and uncommunicative. But troubled. Prescribed Xanax. Wants Friday appointment. UGH!*

As often as I read those words, they didn't really tell me much. I was eager to collect a *lot* more information about the case, as much to address my own uncertainties as to get to know her. I had developed some intake forms (actually I borrowed and adapted them from an agency where I had been working previously) that followed standard protocol, asking questions about presenting symptoms, prior family and medical history, lifestyle activities, current functioning, as well as provided informed consent documents. This is standard operating procedure and the way I had been trained and supervised in order to assist in differential diagnosis and treatment planning. After all, *every* doctor's office and mental health facility asks patients to fill out forms once they check in for an initial appointment.

I was quite curious how my new client would fill in the blanks, so I carefully attached the forms to a clipboard, stuck a pen underneath the metal clip, and began to rock back and forth in my chair, continuing to stare at the clock. Precisely 6 minutes before the appointed time I heard the door to the waiting room open and close. Actually I *felt* the door slam shut with a finality that seemed to shake the walls, which reminded me to get the damn thing adjusted. There were just so many little details to take care of in starting a practice from scratch that I'd never considered before. As a salaried employee of public institutions thus far in my life, I'd never needed to actually depend on outside income in order to earn a living. I was clearly way over my head.

I wondered whether I should wait until the exact time of our scheduled session or whether it would seem like I was too anxious if I greeted her earlier. Should I give her the forms now, a few minutes ahead of time, so we could start the session on time? Or maybe the time she spent filling out the forms counted on the clock? I found this all so confusing.

I decided it was better to greet her right away even if it seemed like I was overanxious. After all, she was anxious too, wasn't she? That's what her doctor had told me and why she was actually consulting me in the first place. And it felt like there was so much at stake for me. I was desperate to increase my caseload. I was beginning to wonder whether this was ever going to pan out.

I opened the door to the waiting room to find a woman who looked older than her chronological age, to use the parlance of the intake and mental status review that I was soon to begin. She looked up at me for a moment but then quickly looked away. Skittish indeed, I thought.

"Hi. I'm Dr. Kottler," I said in my most soothing, reassuring voice. "I'll be with you in a few minutes, but before then could you please fill out these forms?" I hesitated for a moment because she still wasn't making much eye contact. "It will only take a few minutes and then we'll get started." Another reassuring smile.

I retreated back to my office to pretend that I had something else to do besides wait for her to complete the questionnaires. I wished I could play with the new flute to occupy myself but figured that the whispery, discordant sounds I could produce thus far might sound pretty strange coming through the door. During my compulsive preparations, I'd practiced filling out the forms myself just to estimate how long it would take to complete them. Under 10 minutes was my best guess. So I waited. And waited. Then I felt a slight shudder in the walls, as if a door had been carefully opened and closed. Or maybe it was just a premonition.

But I had this terrifying thought: *What if she just left? What if she walked out once I left her alone?*

I tiptoed up to the door to the waiting room, slowly and carefully prying it open for a peek outside, and found to my horror that my new client—my brand new referral—had fled! The clipboard and forms were sitting on her vacant chair. For some reason, all I could think of was that the pen was missing: She took my pen! But then I noticed that it had simply fallen underneath her chair. I felt this hysterical giggle building up in my throat as I thought to myself, *Well, thank goodness I still have my pen!*

I lifted up the clipboard and saw scrolled in big, heavy, bold letters across the first page of the intake forms a handwritten note: "SORRY, BUT I CAN'T GO THROUGH WITH THIS."

I could feel my chest constrict. For a moment, I wondered whether I was going to be the one with a panic attack. I wanted to just sit down on the floor and cry. I had been counting so much on this client being the turning point, the one that signaled that things were finally looking up. Instead, I just lost one fifth of my caseload. I felt so discouraged that I wanted to give up. How would I pay my bills? How would I support my family? How would I ever get this practice on a solid footing?

I decided, in that moment, leaning against one of those flimsy walls for support, that I would never, *ever* lose a client again by failing to first engage that person in a relationship before collecting the information that I thought was usually collected. I decided that I didn't really need—or even want—to know anything about the case or the client's background until I first got to spend time with that person and form my own impressions. I didn't want to read background information, or even know what others thought, until such time that we had established some kind of alliance, some basis for trust. In retrospect, it seems ridiculous to me that we would ask clients to supply all of this incredibly personal information about themselves before they really knew who we were and that we were actually worthy of these very private data. As I reviewed my forms I realized that I was asking perfect strangers to confess their medical history, family history, medications and illicit drugs they were consuming, sleep and eating habits, sexual preferences, legal problems, previous suicidal ideation or suicide attempts, and on and on—just the kinds of things that almost anyone would be reluctant to disclose to a stranger, even a health professional. I know this flies in the face of standard practice in any medical or mental health facility, in which patients are routinely required to supply all kinds of personal details before they are allowed to meet with a health care professional. But just because this was the most convenient and efficient system didn't mean that it was really in the client's best interests or even advantageous for a future helping relationship.

Secrets and Best Practices During First Contact

There are all kinds of research, in so many different contexts, on the critical importance of the first few seconds of a first impression during an initial meeting. Whether formed by the firmness of a handshake, a quick assessment of appearance, or unconscious readings of microexpressions, such first readings become indelible. Although most of the time counselors feel absolutely overwhelmed and flooded to gather as much information as possible, what is often lost in this process is attention to the most important secret of all, which is to solidify an alliance that makes everything else that follows possible.

We have our own agenda and lists. Identify the chief complaint (not to mention the dozen other related or corollary concerns and issues). Collect a personal history, including physical, emotional, cognitive, and interpersonal functioning. Review functioning in a variety of domains, including work, school, and leisure pursuits. Explore lifestyle choices and behavior. Check out family dynamics. Conduct a mental status exam. Determine any dependency on substances or alcohol. Assess for suicide risk. Check out favored coping strategies. Identify signature strengths and resources. Find out what's been working already and what has consistently failed. Explore existing support systems—or the lack thereof. Plan a treatment strategy. Take voluminous notes so you can actually recall these important details. Oh yeah, and also complete all these tasks in a single session.

I actually used to have a cheat sheet hidden on my lap so I could remember the 20 tasks that my supervisor required me to complete during any first session. I was required to begin by checking out the client's expectations for the sessions so I could then correct unrealistic goals. The list continued all the way through to the last item, for which I was required to negotiate a homework assignment for the next session. I was so anxious that I might forget something that I taped the list to my refrigerator so I could memorize every item before my clients caught me looking at my reminder notes.

Finally, I eventually boiled everything down to a handful of questions that reduced all the overwhelming goals to just a few critical areas. The questions were framed in such a manner to emphasize tentativeness, uncertainty, hypothesis testing, and relative caution so as not to foreclose too early on all kinds of other data that would likely come into play much later. I realize of course that this structure for a first session looks very different from what is usually offered. But remember, my secret is to solicit only enough material to get started in a modest way (unless we are talking about *very* brief counseling of only a single session or two) so that you can also focus on building a solid alliance.

1. What is the client's *story?*
2. What is the client's *experience?*
3. What does the client *believe* is going on?
4. What *seems* to be happening?
5. What is the consensual name for this?
6. What *else* could it be?
7. What has the client already tried?
8. What has been working so far?
9. What strategy or approach *might* work best?

You will notice of course that all these questions are offered tentatively so as to permit as much flexibility and adaptability as possible. I try to avoid forming too many assumptions as well as to refrain from thinking in terms of traditional diagnostic language. I usually prefer to avoid looking at *any* background information or hearing anything from a referral source prior to seeing a client, which is the exact opposite of how I was originally trained. I want to first listen to the client's version of the story and the events he or she believes led up to it *before* I review any files, information, questionnaires, or previous data or test results. I want to be able to concentrate first on the connection between us.

Frankly, even after 40 years of practice, and having seen thousands of clients, I *still* feel anxious when I meet a new client. I start to panic because I feel so flooded. I question whether I can really help this person. I always feel lost and uncertain. So rather than trying to do too much, I take a deep breath and just concentrate on the absolute basics. I may question initially the viability of what I can do, but I also trust the process: I know, almost without doubt, that if we can negotiate a good relationship, good things will follow.

A Cherished Secret

I learned a secret from that experience with the client mentioned above, one that I have never forgotten, and have altered my behavior ever since. Whether in the role of a teacher, supervisor, or counselor, I always try to connect with clients first before asking them to complete any paperwork. I've learned over time to have them fill out the forms *after* our initial meeting so that we have the opportunity to get to know each other first. This might not seem like such a big deal, simply moving the paperwork to the end of a session, but it symbolizes to me one of the most important lessons I've ever learned: that relationships are *everything* in our work and that the rest falls into line after we've first taken care of the alliance.

This secret has influenced not only the way I structure my sessions with new clients but also the way I do everything else in my life and work. For many years I have taught an Introduction to Counseling class, with a huge cohort of 65 new students each year. I am saddled with the responsibility of covering all the accreditation requirements for the course as well as all the content that is required. In addition, whenever some new requirement is mandated by a licensing board or accrediting body, it is often just stuck into the Intro course as part of a collection of things that don't seem to be covered elsewhere. As you are aware, the first class session of any course usually involves reviewing the syllabus; discussing the assignments, requirements, grading, and appropriate behavior; and answering all the little questions that students have: "Does the cover page count in the pagination?" "Can we write more than eight pages for the assignments, or is that the limit?" "Is it okay if I have to miss a class because of a prior commitment before I was admitted into the program?"

It's not that these questions aren't important to students, because they do represent examples of their extreme apprehension, fear of failure, and confusion about what is expected. But what that (prospective) client taught me so long ago is that these administrative details can be addressed *after* we have established some kind of relationship with each other first. As much as new students (or clients) are anxious about how things will work and what is expected of them, things become so much easier when we have first created some kind of connection with each other.

Each year I look out across the audience of eager, apprehensive faces, their fingertips poised above their keyboards waiting to record every detail that may be required. In a soft voice I ask them to close all their devices or put down their pens. They immediately look puzzled, then even more anxious, wondering, *Now what? What is the guy doing? I just got here and already he's messing with my head.*

"I want you to look around the room," I tell them. "Go on! I'm serious. Turn around in your seat and check out all the people in this room. Take your time. Try to make eye contact with as many people as you can."

There is nervous giggling, and I can hear snide comments that they think are private. Eventually they turn back around and stare at me with a certain defiance, anxious to get back to work and start taking notes.

"What if I told you that your future closest friends are sitting in this room right now, those whom you will know for the rest of your life? What if I suggested to you that there are people in this room you have not yet even met but who will get to know you as much as, or better than, any friend you've had before? What if I mentioned to you that almost every year, someone meets his or her future roommate, officemate, or partner for the first time in this room?"

Of course the students smile indulgently and shake their heads. I can see a few even roll their eyes. And yet, time after time, when I see these same students a year later, or by the time they are ready to graduate, this prediction has indeed come true. Everything in our profession, and in life for that matter, is about relational connections, especially the kind of deep, trusting, caring relationships in which you feel safe to admit your foibles and weaknesses. Over time I have come to see my job as not only imparting information, teaching concepts and theories, and helping to develop a professional identity but also establishing and maintaining the kinds of bonds with, among, and between everyone in the room such that it feels safe to explore new ideas, critically examine existing ones, and take the kinds of risks that lead to enduring growth and change. This means that it makes no sense whatsoever that I would make a first impression by talking about all the details, rules, and requirements that lead to increased anxiety and doubt. Of course such parameters, boundaries, and guidelines must be covered before clients leave that first session, but that client who fled my office still reminds me about which priorities matter most.

As I mentioned, I have applied this lesson to almost every facet of my life. I remember doing a workshop many years ago, when I was first playing with this idea of relational engagement as a major priority. Not surprisingly, while I waited for the participants to arrive, I nervously paced the hallway, wondering whether I would beguile the audience or lose them entirely. The organizer of the workshop, observing my manic energy, remarked to me that the previous presenter had managed his own anxiety by following a ritual that seemed quite strange at the time. He had removed his shoes and socks and walked around the room before everyone arrived, reporting to the curious onlookers that this helped him get a sense of the space so he could feel comfortable.

I thought that was pretty interesting, not because it appealed to me at all but rather because it seemed so irrelevant to my needs. I could care less about the space. It didn't really matter to me where we were so much as who was in the room. All I cared about was how the audience members would respond to me—and one another. So taking what I had learned and incorporated into my way of being, I decided that the most important thing to set the stage for what would follow, plus calm me down, was to find a way to engage each person in the room before we even started. So I positioned myself at the doorway as people arrived, greeting each participant with a smile, a handshake, a touch on the shoulder, or even a brief conversation. Once I was about to begin the program and looked around the room, it felt to me like I already knew them in some small way—and they knew a little about me. I felt more at ease, more willing to take risks, more open to experimenting and going with the flow instead of sticking with an agenda that, although meticulously planned, might not be appropriate or relevant given who was in the room and what they wanted most.

So that is one of my most cherished professional secrets that guides my life and work. I recognize that systems, procedures, and institutional norms exist as safeguards and standards of practice, but I have found ways to meet their needs without compromising the uniquely personal ways in which we connect with others. For me, that has been true with respect to not only the way I counsel and teach and supervise but also, I hope you notice, the way I write.

What follows in the subsequent chapters are not only the secrets I have developed, gleaned, borrowed, adapted, and held dear to me but also those I've collected from many masters in the field whom I have been privileged to know. Some of them may not fit your own style, context, personality, preferences, values, client population, or way of being, but my hope is that they will stimulate your own thinking and remind you of tough lessons that have changed the ways you work and live.

CHAPTER 2

Admitting You're Lost

This confession is one of my biggest secrets of all: that some of the time, much of the time, maybe even most of the time, I really don't understand what's going on. I know that sounds rather harsh, if not downright inaccurate. After all, we are trained experts. We are masters of diagnostic assessment and evidence-supported treatments. Clearly we know what we are doing, especially because most of our clients do so much better after our care. It has been estimated that anywhere from 75% to 90% of those who seek our counsel end up satisfied with the result.

What I'm admitting, however, isn't that I don't believe I have a handle on what is happening with my clients and what they most need to get better but rather that my level of confidence in this assessment is considerably less than certainty. On a scale of 1 to 10, how positive are you, beyond any doubt whatsoever, that *your* deep understanding of your client's world is absolutely accurate? Or to say that differently, what would you guess the probability is that your grasp of a client's background, needs, interests, condition, symptoms, diagnosis, and life story is entirely on target?

I so vividly recall during my training days when I would sit in on case conferences with supervisors and senior staff, including an assortment of mental health professionals from psychiatric nurses and psychiatrists to psychologists, social workers, and support personnel. I was one of only two interns who identified professionally as a counselor because this was during the days before licensure in most states. Each of us was allotted precisely 15 minutes to present a case, describing the person's mental status, complaints, and symptoms and other information based on a single intake interview. Then it was a free-for-all, in which the various doctors and supervisors would chime in with their diagnoses and recommended treatment plans. But the truly baffling part of this process for me was the utter certainty with which these older doctors would offer their assessments. "This is clearly a case of . . ." one psychiatrist would announce. "I respectfully disagree," another would chime in, and then proceed, with equal authority and confidence, to state that some other phenomenon was in evidence. A half dozen of them would debate and battle among themselves, all the while my head was spinning with increased confusion. It wasn't just that they all seemed so articulate and omnipotent in their pronouncements, it was that none of them could seem to fathom being wrong. All I could do was take meticulous notes and then try to sort out later what I should do next. Usually this took the form of basically ignoring most of what was offered and instead just relying on the client's own best judgment of where to go next.

Wandering in the Dark

The experience of being a counselor is often one of operating in the dark with sometimes the barest glimmer of shadows that we can make out. Clients often obfuscate, exaggerate, or even downright lie in whatever they tell us. Whatever assumptions we make about a case, we know that they are only hypotheses that have yet to be fully supported. Each of us has spent decades living with ourselves and yet we sometimes can't figure out what *we* want or need most, so how could we possibly know such things about someone with whom we spend less than an hour each week?

"I've been feeling so anxious lately," a client reveals during an early session.

"Yes, you've mentioned that several times. When were you first aware that these feelings were becoming disturbing to you?"

"I'm not really sure. I mean, I've been under a lot of pressure lately at work and all. And I've told you that in a few months we are expecting our first child."

"You also mentioned something about your mother being anxious much of her life, a condition you both share."

"True. And I've also been working with an endocrinologist to help regulate my thyroid function. The meds haven't been helpful lately."

"So there's a lot of possible explanations for the symptoms you've been having related to your family history, stress on the job, becoming a new father, plus your hormone imbalance."

"Yeah, I know all that. So what do *you* think is the cause, and what should I do about it?"

Good question. In fact, *great* question. And it's not as if the counselor won't provide a somewhat evasive answer to buy some time. The truth is that there's really no way to know for sure what might be contributing to the problem, or even which combination of precipitating events, biosocial factors, and family dynamics might be most at fault. So we fake it as best we can.

The truly remarkable thing is that it often doesn't matter much the extent to which we have the clearest possible understanding of the client's situation and complaints. There are times when it feels like we are both just wandering around, lost in the dark, trying to remain composed in the face of such confusing and complex obstacles all around us.

As disorienting as it might be to admit that sometimes we feel lost, what strikes me as far worse are those among us who claim (or pretend) that they know *exactly* what they're doing almost all the time. They issue proclamations about their clients as if they were indelible truths. They speak with complete authority about the way things are, without the slightest hint that there could be alternative realities. Far worse, they would rarely if ever admit that they are clueless or lost.

For an earlier project, Jon Carlson and I once interviewed prominent and famous therapists about their failures and mistakes. I will never forget one such theoretician who had long been a hero of mine. I was excited to talk to him, given that his books had been so valuable to me during my student days. Even though he had agreed to participate in our project, after we asked him to share one of his most memorable failures, he stalled for a bit and then claimed that he really couldn't think of an instance in which he had ever failed as a therapist. I was so dumbfounded by his response that I almost missed the follow-up: "And furthermore," he added, "I consider any therapist who does admit to failure to be incompetent."

There are of course good reasons for denying our fallibility. There are also practitioners among us who are not only less than perfectly competent but also unwilling to admit their mistakes—and thus unable or unwilling to learn from them. I usually require beginning counseling students to interview professionals in the field, and one of the questions they are required to ask is related to a story about failure and the lessons learned. One such student reported, "Some of the responses I heard were so wince-worthy that I didn't even mention them in my paper. When I asked one counselor what theory she favored, she asked me what I meant by a 'theory,' and she genuinely didn't seem to know what that was." Another practitioner she interviewed disclosed the names of her clients, some of whom the student knew. In each case, the counselor didn't even seem to be aware that these were serious lapses.

We all have stories like this, about counselors who are not only incompetent or clueless but also dangerous. They don't learn from their mistakes because of their unwillingness to admit that they ever make errors in judgment. I spoke with a counselor recently who was bragging about a recent case in which he was seeing the client pro bono, for no fee whatsoever. When I mentioned that there is some evidence that it is often useful for clients to invest even a minimal fee in their treatment, if just a few dollars, he scoffed at that and then mentioned that he often loaned his clients money—for a reasonable interest rate of course.

When You Feel Awkward and Lost

Most of us were first introduced to the profession either through our own experiences as a client or else by watching a demonstration of a session on video. In the latter case, we sat spellbound while watching the seemingly effortless magic taking place before our eyes. The client, usually some hopeless case who has already consulted a variety of other practitioners without success, proceeds to describe symptoms so severe and intractable that it is amazing that he or she manages to get out of bed in the morning. But then the master counselor goes to work with some incantation or signature technique—and voila! The person is cured and lives happily ever after.

Watching these demonstrations, or hearing about cases from supervisors or instructors, only solidified the belief that counseling sessions are extremely well-organized, coherent affairs, meticulously planned and artistically executed. Clients are almost always cooperative and responsive, and the counselor appears perfectly in control of the proceedings. The deep dark secret of course is that even the so-called masters, those whose videos or demonstrations we adore and try to emulate, rarely perform so well when off stage. Just like the rest of us, they sometimes feel awkward and lost.

When Jon Carlson, who produced more than 300 demonstration videos with the most notable practitioners of the past century, first invited me to make a film of my own demonstrating my theoretical approach in action, I was flattered of course but also terrified. First of all, I wasn't sure what my personal theory was called, given my flexibility and continual evolution. Second, I was absolutely certain there was no way my counseling approach would ever look as polished and organized as those I've admired throughout my career; I prefer to follow where the client leads, an often chaotic dance initially, rather than present a prearranged structure. Sometimes we start in the middle and work our way to the ends. Other times we jump all over the place until many of the pieces fall together. But one thing that I was fairly certain about was that I didn't want to contribute to the myth that counseling usually looks like the demonstrations we have been taught to follow.

Once arriving at the studio, I was surprised to learn that I would be expected to see three different clients so they could pick the best one. "But each of my sessions is always different," I explained. "Besides, I'd really prefer to pick the *worst* one so students could see what *really* happens behind closed doors when clients are uncooperative, resistant, or sometimes even mute."

So here's a secret I'm going to share with you that few people know. Jon Carlson explained to me that although many of the most famous therapists and counselors are truly exceptional at their craft, there are also several (and I'm not mentioning names) who are horrifyingly awkward and graceless. They may have been brilliant theoreticians and excellent writers, perhaps even charismatic teachers, but that didn't necessarily mean that they were all that skilled at practicing their own ideas when it counted most with clients. In some cases, they became researchers, instructors, or writers because they realized how much they disliked actually seeing clients who may not have been willing to show them the reverence they expected and demanded.

Carlson further disclosed that he had even had to ask a few individuals to return to the studio a second time to see an additional three clients in order to find one that was suitable for public viewing. So it turns out that truly exceptional counselors are not those who have received the most attention and adulation but rather include those among us working in relative obscurity. I truly hope that this confession bolsters and validates your own experience—that no matter how well prepared you might be, how well trained and supervised, how poised and confident, it is still part of our collective journey to embrace our uncertainty.

Most of our sessions rarely, if ever, look like those demonstrations by the masters: They are often chaotic, confusing, awkward, and by no means pretty. They usually involve a period of negotiation—about roles but also about what is covered and how it is best handled. It is not only expected but also common that there will be a certain amount of tension, conflict, and disagreement about these issues. There are inevitable misunderstandings and miscommunications. Each of the participants struggles to connect with the other, often at cross-purposes. The result is often a conversation that is both disjointed and confusing.

"So I was telling you about the problems that keep coming up at work and what a jerk my boss is . . ."

"Yes, but I was wondering how this is connected to the family issues that first brought you here. You had said that you . . ."

"Really? *That's* why you think I'm here?"

"Isn't it?"

"Ah, not exactly."

"What then?"

"What do you mean?"

"No, what do *you* mean?"

This would sound almost comical if it weren't actually so familiar to us in the early, awkward stage of getting to know each other and figure out a consensual agenda. I don't mean to imply that you must feel as awkward and lost as I do during the first session or two, but this is how counseling usually begins for me—with a certain amount of tentativeness and confusion. And it looks nothing like the demonstrations we have seen that have been carefully rehearsed and edited or the case examples that are presented that always seem so clear and controlled.

I recall as a student trying to reconcile the stories my instructors would share in class about cases that seemed so complex and challenging and clients who were on the verge of self-destruction; because of the brilliant interventions, there was always a happy ending. I would look around the room and everyone seemed to be soaking the lesson up, but such anecdotes only made me feel more inadequate, that I'd never be able to function nearly as well. Truthfully, I still feel that way.

Behind the Curtain

Many professions prefer not to reveal what actually goes on behind the curtain. We are rarely offered a glimpse of what is actually involved in all the details that go into a successful effort, whether it is passing a piece of legislation, demonstrating a magic trick, negotiating a legal contract, completing a surgical procedure, or conducting a counseling session. We hear about what happened in sanitized, abbreviated form. We see the result with limited explanation. And we are shielded from all the struggles, obstacles, and setbacks along the way.

Most of the time we may pretend we know what's going on, but, if we are honest, it sometimes feels like we are riding on a runaway wagon and we aren't sure who exactly is holding onto the reins and steering the damn thing. We keep hitting ruts in the road—or losing the path altogether.

Let me invite you into my head during a typical session, with my internal thoughts italicized.

> *Client:* So I was telling you last time about my cousin's longstanding problem with weed and how he's been pressuring me to get high with him more often *[You were? I don't remember it quite that way. You were admitting that you were the one smoking too much.]* And Flip was saying how I should . . . *[Wait a minute. Who is Flip? He never mentioned a Flip before. Sounds like a dog's name, but he mentioned that Flip was "saying" something, so he/she/it must be able to speak.]* . . . stop being so hard on myself and just chill. Know what I mean? *[Absolutely not.]*
>
> *Me:* What you seem to be saying is that you feel caught between the pressure from several different sources. *[I don't even know why I said that. But I had to say something.]*
>
> *Client:* Yeah. Right. *[Right? You don't understand what I just said either.] [Uh oh. He's looking at me, waiting for me to do something or say something. Or maybe he's just thinking what he wants to say next.]*
>
> *Me:* Um. So we were talking last time also about this pattern in your life in which some of your struggles relate directly to the ways your parents used to treat you whenever you made a mistake or were less than perfect. *[I'm not sure whether that's true or not but it sure sounded good. Now I'm thinking . . .]*

Well, you get the idea. And this sort of internal dialogue may even be familiar to you at times. I'm not implying that this is always normative, but certainly in the beginning of most counseling relationships we are often struggling to get a handle on what might really be happening and what the best strategy or course of action might be given that we have so many possible options at our disposal. Is it too early to confront the client? Should I let this rambling story continue or interrupt? A role play might bring things into better focus. I wonder whether it might be time to consider ruling out any organic issues that could be contributing to the symptoms?

We are part of a profession in which people expect us to have clear, definitive answers. We fight for respect among other health professionals who often refer to us as "shrinks" or sometimes "quacks" who allegedly use placebos, a magic wand, and mere good intentions to pretend to help others. Among various medical specialties, psychiatrists are treated as know-nothings who command the least regard among their colleagues compared to surgeons or internists who actually *do* something.

If we are truly honest with ourselves, we must admit that there are times when we are just winging it, just coasting along, pretending we know where things are going when in fact we are just wandering around until we can figure out what's really going on. There are so many of examples of this that we just take for granted and accept as part of the job.

What Is Real? What Is Truth?

A client tells us something that we know isn't really accurate: "I had a happy childhood." "I'm doing really fine right now, thanks for asking." "I'm not the one with the problem; it's others that don't understand what's going on." "I don't have a drug problem." Do we challenge the client or not?

Uncertainty and Confusion

Someone has been telling a long, rambling story for more than 10 minutes, and you have no idea what the point is or where it is going: "I think my teachers just don't get me, you know? The math homework, anyway, it just didn't make sense. She told us to do one thing but then graded us on binomials, which we never really covered in class. There was this one time I was talking to Myra, who sits next to me, and she was saying that her dad is some bigtime equity dealer and he flunked algebra when he was in school and yet he makes millions. I guess he was some kind of genius or something. Where was I?"

We may very well wonder the same thing.

Flooded With Choices

There's been interminable silence in a session, and you can't figure out what it means. Finally, after what feels like several minutes but is probably a fraction of that time, you ask a question to prompt some response. Again the client just stares at his feet. Next you try asking a direct question: "I'm wondering if you are really struggling right now putting your thoughts into words?" You see a slight head shake that you can't quite decipher. Is he saying yes or no?

Now you are left to wonder: Is the client being resistant? Is he just thinking about something important? Is he waiting for you to do something else? Should you let it go or rescue him? And if you do jump in to fill the space, would it be better to reflect what is happening in this moment, the meaning of the pause, or perhaps go back to what was said earlier in the session? Would it be best to interpret some possible resistance at this point or just ignore that and stay with the client's readiness and apparent reluctance? The list of options only grows once you consider that one single choice doesn't appear obvious or optimal.

Feeling Overwhelmed

Once we hear the initial narrative of any new client, we are almost always struck by the complexity of a life, its background and context, all the factors that may come into play. And as much as we might like to hone in on a single symptom, problem, or issue, possibly dozens of different influences and interconnected factors are involved. A seemingly straightforward presenting problem—seeking help and support after a relationship loss—eventually reveals a host of other difficulties that may or may not be relevant or related. The breakup occurred immediately after a seemingly meaningless dispute about whose turn it was to select a movie to watch. But then you witness evidence of impulsivity during sessions, a propensity to be argumentative. You hear about a succession of other relationships that ended rather abruptly. You learn that "occasionally" this client likes to drink "a little." And oh yeah, she is on medication for some undisclosed medical condition. You notice visible hand tremors, and you're not sure what those are about. And yes, of course the person wants an instant diagnosis and cure even though she has no idea what's going on and marginal capacity for insight. This client has so many issues and problems you don't know where to begin to help dig her out of the muck.

Diagnostic Decisions

After presenting his story, a client asks for a diagnosis and wonders how long it will take for a cure. On some level, you might wonder how the heck you are supposed to come up with a definitive answer, given how little you really know and understand about this person after just a few hours. After all, he has been living with himself his whole life, and he doesn't seem to know or understand much.

You wonder whether these symptoms represent a cry for help rather than a more serious underlying disorder. This is especially challenging when the client just doesn't fit anything you've ever encountered before, anything you've ever heard of before.

Reconciling the Need for Definitive Answers With the Realities of Uncertainty

Clearly one of our most difficult challenges is to address the client's need to understand what is going on, why the problem persists, how and why it developed, and what the best course of action is to resolve the issues. In addition, the insurance-based system and organizations within which we operate demand that we provide clear diagnostic assessments that include cogent descriptions of symptomology, etiological causes, and clinical labels for the presenting condition. We must take these tasks seriously if we wish to continue functioning as professionals.

And yet we also try to be honest with ourselves that although we must function within this context and system, and provide required labels and definitive treatment plans framed in the language of expertise, we must remind ourselves that in any professional domain, certainty is an illusion. Rather than apologizing for sometimes feeling lost and uncertain, I prefer to frame this is as a valuable trait signaling courage. It does indeed take courage to be a counselor, to practice a craft that delves so deeply into life's most puzzling questions that include exploring motives underlying behavior, sorting out the reasons why people do the things they do, and searching for meaning and purpose in daily life.

Whereas our medical colleagues have all kinds of impressive technology to assist with their diagnostic decisions—magnetic resonance imaging, electrocardiograms, biopsies, implantable devices, molecular sampling, computed tomography, ultrasound, blood and urine tests, as well as physical exams using all kinds of instruments—we rely primarily on observation and conversation to collect relevant information. Sure we may use assessment instruments, but their reliability isn't quite in the same realm as providing precise, quantifiable blood counts or three-dimensional scans of the brain. So we do the best we can by tempering our limited scientific tools with the unique human gifts of systematic observation, clinical assessment, intuition, and conversational discourse that are the hallmarks of our profession. These are the tools that allow us to enter our clients' world and, if nothing else, help them to feel that they are not alone in their suffering.

We tend to get into trouble when we put clients into diagnostic boxes, start to think of them as labels, like a child who *is* a developmental disorder, autistic spectrum disorder, or (a new popular one) disruptive mood dysregulation disorder. Such labels do appease our own anxiety to a certain extent; they reassure us that there is a name for what we are encountering and often suggest particular treatment strategies that are empirically supported for that particular problem configuration. But as much as they help us to feel less lost, diagnostic entities sometimes also back us into a corner, limiting the creative and more flexible ways we might conceptualize behavior. The same thing might also be said with respect to conceptual paradigms and theoretical structures, a subject I take up in the next chapter.

CHAPTER 3

Theories Are Simply Flexible Frameworks

Theories represent organizing frameworks of knowledge that help us to make sense of the world, people's behavior, and the best options for helping others to make needed changes in their lives. They rely pretty much on some general principles, followed by coherent, testable propositions, that are applied to a variety of situations and contexts, whether justified or not.

Thus, theories are extraordinarily helpful and critical to practitioners of any craft, as they help make meaning of situations. A plumber would offer a theory about why a pipe may be blocked, just as a counselor would formulate assumptions about why one child in a family is experiencing major trauma while others have recovered rather quickly from abuse. Theories thus serve the purpose of providing a blueprint for action, narrowing choices that appear most reasonable and applicable given the information available. They direct our actions to where they might do the most good based on a synthesis of variables, influences, and factors that may come into play.

Of course such an overarching model is important as the primary means by which to (try to) understand our clients, much less help them most effectively. But it is also important to recognize just how limited any theory can be when applied to such a diverse population of clientele, each of whom has distinctly different characteristics, issues, preferences, and experiences. Many of the popular theories of counseling and psychotherapy were originally developed based on client populations that were fairly homogeneous and not exactly relevant today. For instance, just as many of the most influential psychological experiments were conducted with convenience samples of college students, Sigmund Freud's theories of psychoanalysis were based on a very specific sample of privileged, Viennese women in the later 19th century. Likewise, many of the prevailing traditional theoretical paradigms were hardly tested with the kinds of culturally diverse, economically disadvantaged clients that we see today.

The reality is that very few counselors still practice any theory in its pure, unadulterated form. In the studies I mentioned in a previous chapter, in which Jon Carlson and I interviewed some of the most famous theorists in the field, such as William Glasser, Albert Ellis, Jay Haley, Jim Bugental, and Arnold Lazarus (notice of course that these are mostly White men), I was astounded by several of them who, when asked to discuss their most creative session or their most memorable case, described an intervention or strategy that didn't seem remotely related to their own theory. When I asked a few of them to account for this, the reaction was simply a shrug and confession: "Oh, I moved on from that years ago."

In other words, by the time an idea or model is developed, tested, applied, published, and disseminated and gains attention, years if not decades have passed. Furthermore, in today's professional climate it is commonplace for prominent theorists to share panel discussions together, collaborate on projects, and engage in social interactions and friendships. It is impossible to avoid being influenced by another's ideas, even if you may appear to passionately disagree in public. I recall a number of conversations on panels that took place behind the curtain in which theorists exchanged ideas with one another, grappled with differences in the ways they accounted for phenomena, and queried one another regarding how and why they explained things in a particular way. Such discussions clearly lead to far more integrative practice than one would imagine.

Likewise, behind closed doors most of us are far more pragmatic, flexible, and eclectic than we might believe—or claim to be to others. One cannot be exposed to some intriguing idea or inventive practice without wishing to somehow adapt and integrate it in a useful way to better help one's own clients. Almost every time I've watched some exceptional clinician in action, demonstrating a skill or strategy that I've never encountered before, I've tried to figure out a way to make it my own—even if it is grounded in a theoretical paradigm that is foreign to me.

Theories Are Stories to Explain Things

Accreditation bodies such as the Council for Accreditation of Counseling and Related Educational Programs, American Psychological Association, American Association for Marriage and Family Therapy, and National Association of Social Workers, as well as state licensing boards, now mandate particular requirements that supersede any single theoretical paradigm and instead focus on consensual standards and evidence-based practices. Generic helping skills are now the norm. Every practitioner learns the same basic interventions for reflecting feelings, responding to content, summarizing, setting goals, and so on. Every counselor now borrows ideas from a variety of approaches, depending on the client, context, and even mood. We now have virtually universal consensus on certain standards of practice and ethical guidelines to which we all subscribe, regardless of our theoretical orientation. We basically agree on most of the diagnostic entities that are used to assess and classify the problems that are brought to us—even if in broad strokes when considering mood disorders versus adjustment reactions or personality disorders versus organic/somatic complaints. Most of us are also in agreement about particular best practices—that it's a good idea to have solid boundaries in counseling relationships, or that personal and professional relationships with clients are potentially problematic, or that insight alone is often not enough to promote change. Another example includes all the different ways in which various theories introduce various ways of conceptualizing problems in more constructive, empowering terms, whether it is called interpretation, disputing beliefs, reframing, alternative outcomes, or restorying. They may each use different terms to describe the intervention, but they all help people to think in more proactive, empowering ways about problems that feel quite limiting.

Particular theories also represent moments frozen in time depending on the knowledge and technology available during that era. It was once considered a legitimate, honorable theory to diagnose witches by tying their hands and feet together and then throwing them in a deep pond: If they managed to survive, they would be burned at the stake; if they drowned, they were innocent but very dead. Similarly, more than 100 years ago, the prevailing therapeutic system was animal magnetism, in which clients were subjected to all kinds of mumbo-jumbo to heal their perceived blood imbalances.

Considering how quickly technology and best practices are evolving, it is even more critical to consider the limited shelf life of any theory that is based on obsolete knowledge. It was only a few years ago that traumatic stress debriefing was the rage for any and all emergency and military personnel who survived some catastrophic event. The theory stated that helping them to get in touch with and express their feelings in group settings would be a good idea—but it was later discovered that for some people, some of the time, that made things significantly worse. Posttraumatic reactions—both debilitating and growth inducing—are now handled much differently in light of new theories.

All prevailing counseling theories today are organized around a series of assumptions and beliefs that are often at odds with one another. Some theories focus on the past, whereas others hone in on the present or future. There are also passionate disagreements regarding whether we should privilege feelings over thoughts or thoughts over behavior. Similarly, some theories point to goals that are general, others quite specific, and still others process oriented. Some are highly active and directive in prescribing the counselor's role, whereas others believe that we should allow the client to decide what is best. There is even considerable debate as to whether allegiance to a single theory is really still viable considering that the vast majority of practitioners describe themselves as eclectic, using several different approaches depending on what they encounter and think might work best.

Theories are really just stories to explain things we don't understand. Although some of these narratives are more easily verifiable than others, each one represents a particular slice of reality. And despite the fact that there are estimated to be more than 400 distinctly different theories currently in operation, each one is often presented as The Answer that renders all others obsolete. The infighting within our profession has been downright embarrassing, with proponents of one particular theory seeking to discredit all others. Scant evidence exists to justify such claims that any single theory is far superior to all others in every situation.

There has clearly been a movement toward integration in recent years. Most counselors are willing to use whatever ideas they can beg, borrow, or steal to improve their effectiveness and lead to a breakthrough. It's about flexibility and adaptability to the ever-changing nature of the world, technology, new evidence, and improved data. Thus, so-called evidence-based practices and empirically supported treatments have led the charge to abandon singular theories altogether in lieu of specific targeted treatments that are matched to particular sets of symptoms. As attractive as this might appear to link us more clearly to scientific investigations, the reality is that we desperately need some kind of organizing framework or model to guide our professional behavior and decision making.

Theoretical Purity Is No More

It was Sir Arthur Conan Doyle (under the guise of Sherlock Holmes) who observed the dangers of twisting facts to fit a theory instead of adjusting one's ideas to fit the unique and novel aspects of any singular case. Thus, one of the dangers faced by more experienced counselors is that we think we've seen everything before. A new client walks in the door and immediately we begin the accommodation cognitive process, putting the person into one of our familiar categories, whether a diagnostic entity or a personally subscribed pattern:

- "Here's another parachute mother hoping to swoop in and control every facet of her son's life."
- "So you say you've been having trouble sleeping at night since the accident. Sounds like posttraumatic stress."
- "When you say that your father is always on your case, what you really mean is that he doesn't really appreciate what is most important to you."
- "The symptoms you are describing sound like a pretty classic case of panic disorder."
- "As the middle child in your family you must have frequently felt caught in the middle of conflicts, which explains why you have such difficulty taking a definitive position on so many issues."

Of course each of these assumptions could very well be accurate, at least for some people some of the time. But we tend to get in trouble when we fail to recognize exceptions to the rule. We see clients not as they are but rather as we imagine them to be.

Within the medical profession, doctors are warned about the sorts of cognitive errors that can result from relying too much on clinical algorithms, decision trees, and lists of diagnostic symptoms. This can lead to faulty pattern recognition and coping with uncertainty by filling in the blanks with assumptions, preconceptions, and theoretical suppositions that are actually not in evidence in a particular case.

Ironically, it is embracing our uncertainty and doubts that leads us to put aside a favored theory, at least for a little while, in order to meet clients where they are rather than where we expect them to be. Perhaps the 17th-century English poet John Wilmot said it best when he commented that before he got married, he had six different theories on how best to raise children. "Now," he admitted, "I have six children and no theories."

This may sound wise, but the reality is that we are expected to embrace a particular theoretical paradigm. Licensing exams or comprehensive exams may even require a student or intern to discuss a case within the context of a favored model. We still often teach a theories course as a flavor of the week, in which a dozen of the more popular theories are introduced throughout the semester. Students are expected to learn and understand the basics of a model that would actually take a year or more to even partially comprehend.

Whereas once upon a time there was something called *theoretical purity* in that counselors were expected to learn and follow a single conceptual model during their career and become a true advocate for that singular approach, nowadays the secret is out that almost everyone is integrative in their approach and highly pragmatic in their selection of interventions, depending on the client, situation, presenting complaint, and context. As mentioned earlier, much of this blending of ideas and increased eclecticism resulted from the field's major theorists interacting and collaborating with one another more often. Whether they were aware of it or not, whether they deliberately borrowed one another's ideas or not, each theorist began to sound more and more like the others. As an example, Albert Ellis used to call his approach *rational emotive,* then it became *rational emotive behavioral* once he integrated more behavioral ideas into his previously cognitive model. After being exposed to constructivist language to describe internal processes, Ellis later added some of those features as well, embracing some of the thinking of other cognitive theorists such as Aaron Beck, Judith Beck, Donald Meichenbaum, and others.

In spite of their proclamations of loyalty to a particular conceptual paradigm, the vast majority of counselors operate fairly eclectically. We may prefer to subscribe to a particular model that we believe best describes and explains the nature of change, but the reality is that we also borrow ideas from a variety of other approaches depending on what is most indicated. There is thus often a disconnect between a counselor's espoused beliefs and what he or she actually does behind closed doors with a desperate client. Is there really anyone operating today who does not use role playing, or challenge dysfunctional attitudes, or help people set realistic goals? Who among us does *not* adapt techniques, interventions, or skills from an assortment of counseling approaches?

I'm often linked to existential/relational approaches to counseling; yet if you would watch me in action, you'd be hard pressed to identify a single definitive approach—at least through observation—even though I might be relying on this model inside my head to make sense of what I think might be happening. I will do almost *anything* to get through to a client. It is precisely because I am familiar with so many approaches to counseling that I have such a broad range of options from which to choose. I'd like to think that one secret of most exceptional counselors is that they have collected and developed so many therapeutic options that they can fluidly adapt what they are doing to better serve their clients, especially when they encounter roadblocks.

This begs the question as to why we are still teaching theory courses in graduate school or at least presenting the material by introducing a different model each week. There are few actual true believers who subscribe to and use one exclusive counseling approach for all their clients and in every situation; most of us take the time to combine favorite ideas to create our own customized style that reflects our own unique personality, strengths, preferences, values, and attitudes as well as skillset. So the secret I am outing is that exclusive allegiance to a single theory is somewhat obsolete—except as part of our historical legacy.

Some Notable Figures Chime in With Their Secrets

Michael Yapko is one of the leading proponents of strategic, solution-focused approaches to counseling and therapy. He has been a prominent voice in the movement to use pragmatic, creative, and evidence-based interventions for a variety of issues and problems. He has also been a significant innovative figure applying the hypnotic methods of Milton Erickson as an alternative to more medicalized approaches when treating depression and anxiety.

Yapko actually takes issue with practitioners who become so attached to their theories about why people behave in particular ways: "Somewhere along the way, they manage to lose sight of the fact that their prized theories are simply metaphors for experience." His point is that such theories don't necessarily reflect reality or truth but simply describe propositions that may—or may not—apply to a particular individual. They certainly help us to better understand certain phenomena and ways of being, but he also makes the point that they can block our ability to view things in more useful or creative ways.

Yapko mentions as an example that we may have been exposed to certain concepts like superego or collective unconsciousness, but sometimes we forget that these are metaphoric representations: "You don't really have an 'inner child,'" he says, "that is, unless you are pregnant!"

One of Yapko's most important secrets is this: "Therapists and counselors regularly get lost in their theories trying to explain why people have their problems, perhaps as a result of childhood trauma or a dysfunctional family, instead of truly considering the unique characteristics of individuals and how they actively but unintentionally create their symptoms and circumstances. It's all about how to teach clients to make better choices and decisions."

Yapko believes that overattachment to a theory can often lead to the kind of global thinking and overgeneralizations that limit options, not to mention reinforce the same kind of cognitive errors that brought clients into counseling in the first place. As just one example, he mentions the seemingly benign platitude "He who hesitates is lost." Certainly this is sometimes true. Maybe you could even make a case that it is often a useful guide. But then there are other instances in which the opposite is true: "Fools rush in where angels fear to tread." These sorts of universal rules can promote uncritical acceptance of the status quo, or what is most familiar, instead of looking for exceptions. In addition, they can lead clients to overpersonalize disappointments, to believe that somehow it must be their fault that things didn't work out because the theory must be correct. Yapko says, "They may not realize that the problem is actually caused by a rigid adherence to a belief or philosophy that is counterproductive to the realities of their specific circumstances."

"The therapeutic solution to counter such global thinking," Yapko argues, "is in teaching people to make perceptive distinctions in the service of making better decisions. Thus, it becomes more important to ask *how* someone can learn to make better decisions in a given context than it is to ask *why* they're not already doing so. Not nearly enough clinicians learn to do this *at all,* much less *well,* in my opinion."

Barry Duncan also promotes an alternative conception of theory, its uses, and its limitations. Duncan is one of the premier researchers of counseling outcomes and what best predicts successful and satisfying therapeutic relationships. Working in collaboration with a number of scholars, he has been instrumental in bringing greater attention to systematic efforts on the part of counselors and therapists to solicit ongoing meaningful feedback throughout the process. Like Yapko, he believes that the context of a client's experience is absolutely critical and that allegiance to a single model may cripple a counselor's willingness to adjust strategies to best fit any person's needs. After all, he argues, it is the *client's* perceptions of the problem and situation that matter most. Thus, one of his most invaluable secrets is that it is the client's worldview, his or her map of the territory, that best determines a personalized theory for any given therapeutic relationship.

Duncan has spent his career collecting systematic data and empirical support related to matching client preferences with the theoretical structures and clinical strategies that are actually used. In other words, he is a big fan of asking clients to describe their theories about what they are experiencing and what they think might be most helpful, at least as a starting point. "Asking about and implementing the client's theories does not preclude therapist ideas, suggestions, models, methods, or in any way mean that therapists do not contribute to this shared meaning making. Instead, this speaks to the more collaborative aspects of formulating a plan, with the degree and intensity of counselor input determined by the client's expectations of the counselor's role."

It is by honoring the client's own theory that we are best able to build a more cooperative partnership, one that respects the client's beliefs and priorities rather than privileging those of the counselor. As Duncan says, "Given the frequent hyping of the method of the month, there's a temptation to turn an idea, like the client's theory of change, into one more invariant therapeutic prescription. Prescribe some ritual like finger waving or paradoxical restraint and watch the miracles roll out the office door!"

Duncan is quick to acknowledge that it isn't as if we can simply ask clients what their theory is and expect a complete and accurate answer: "It is more of an emergent reality that unfolds from a conversation structured by the therapist's curiosity about the client's ideas, attitudes, and speculations about change." Duncan's secret then is to remind himself constantly that every client presents with a new and unique theory to learn, which implies an individualized and different kind of relationship and process. To state that more rigorously and carefully: "Counseling can be conceptualized as an idiosyncratic, process-determined synthesis of ideas that culminates in a new theory with explanatory and predictive validity for the client's specific circumstance." This is why it's important to have at our disposal a number of models and therapeutic options. And like Yapko, Duncan agrees that theories are somewhat arbitrary metaphorical accounts of how people *can* change, not the ways that people actually *must* change.

Another influential scholar and practitioner, Jose Cervantes, also shares the belief that many if not most theories are obsolete, especially those that are invented by others and not customized and personalized to reflect one's own unique style. Cervantes often operates in a very unique therapeutic milieu, having specialized in helping undocumented immigrants as well as following the traditions of his indigenous ancestors from Mexico. Honoring his native roots, he is constantly exploring the interconnectedness of all life, encompassing the physical, emotional, cognitive, and spiritual facets of experience.

Reviewing his theoretical allegiances earlier in his career, Cervantes notes that he has at one time or another followed family systems, humanistic, and transpersonal models but has since embraced perspectives that are more amenable to viewing individuals as spiritual beings. He is particularly attracted to the work of healers and mystics who talk about what it means to follow a meaningful life: "I have embraced an understanding that the human experience within the larger scope of life's dilemmas, challenges, and gains is a spiritual journey, a meaningful pathway that is oriented around three universal beliefs: the Law of Karma (all behavior has a corresponding reaction), the Law of Attraction (the body goes wherever the mind flows), and the understanding of Earth as a living being (all life forms have a relationship to each other that supports balance)."

The value that theory offers to Cervantes is not as a prescription for helping or a set of specific guidelines and assumptions that lead to specific therapeutic interventions but rather as a philosophy that helps him to develop a more compassionate heart, greater awareness, respect, and responsibility for the sacredness of each person's life journey. This of course is a very different way to conceptualize and utilize theory, one that permits each of us to develop our own unique voice, our own brand of helping, that not only reflects unique signature strengths but also may be better adapted and customized to the particular needs of any client, with any issue, in almost any context.

CHAPTER 4

Developing Your Own Voice

Early in my life and career, I was a hero/heroine worshipper. I became a groupie for any number of famous figures in our field, most of them now long dead, their theories still sputtering along. Every few years (or even months), I would become attached to a new and different theorist, mentor, supervisor, or author and try to learn and imitate everything I could. As a student, I would sit in awe while listening to a few of my instructors regale us with stories of their exploits and therapeutic adventures. After graduating, I systematically attended the workshops and trainings of all the most famous figures of the era—Virginia Satir, Albert Ellis, B. F. Skinner, William Glasser, the list goes on and on; in each case, friends and colleagues would remark that I actually sounded like them for months afterward. I'm not surprised; I desperately wanted to *be* them. Each time I would fall under the spell of a new and different mentor, I would do my best to imitate them, unconsciously internalizing their manner of speech and style. But what happened along the way was that I lost my own voice: I no longer recognized who I was because I was so busy trying to be someone else.

Every teacher, supervisor, or mentor I've ever had still whispers to me, although after so many years I can no longer identify whether those voices are now internalized as part of my own. Each of the influential figures seemed so absolutely certain about his or her approach, so convinced that it was also the best option for everyone else, including me. I remember times when I might bring up some idea or thought of my own and it was stamped down in lieu of one of the masters I was supposed to follow every step of the way. There were times I'd be sitting in session and hear myself say things that didn't even really belong to me but rather was just my teacher, mentor, or supervisor speaking through me. It's a strange feeling indeed to hear yourself talking and not recognize yourself because you are really just channeling someone else!

I sometimes sat in sessions when a client would make some remark, and I would sit mute and frozen, absolutely overwhelmed with all the voices inside my head instructing me about what to do. I had lost the ability to sort out what I actually believed, much less discover or develop my own way of being as a counselor, because I was busy trying to follow the lead of charismatic mentors. Even as I recognized what I had become—or rather what I had *not* become—I felt powerless to change the pattern. I didn't trust that I knew enough, or was bright and skilled enough, to depart from what others had offered to me. After all, they were important and famous and I was, and would always be, a protégé whose job was not to question the status quo but rather to dutifully follow in their footsteps.

To make matters more difficult, during those rare instances when I might challenge a mentor or supervisor, I felt shamed and ridiculed. How dare I, a mere mortal, question the validity or applicability of an idea? Years went by. Eventually I found myself in positions of authority, standing in front of a classroom, writing a book, presenting a workshop, supervising others, and yet I was still spouting what I'd been told by others rather than speaking my own truth. Or if not truth, at least my long-buried beliefs and ideas.

I'd like to say that there was a single moment of insight, if not a period of inspiration, in which I suddenly recognized my own inauthenticity, threw off the shackles of approval-seeking bondage, and found my own voice, but that's not the secret I'm here to tell. The process of sorting out my own values and beliefs, figuring out what I hold most sacred, and discovering my own style took far longer than I could have imagined.

Conflicts and Arguments That Stifle Individual Voices

Almost everyone in our field has a rather strong opinion about what they do and how they do it. We can become rather passionate and dogmatic at times, convinced that we have discovered the one true path to enlightenment. Our journals, conferences, case conferences, and meetings can become heated at times as we argue with one another about which is the best way to go about our business. I have witnessed fistfights practically break out on panel discussions in which founders of particular theories make the case that their ideas are superior to everyone else's.

I once moderated two successive panel discussions at an international conference with several of the most famous writers in the field of psychotherapy. Each of the participants was granted 10 minutes, after which there was supposed to be interactive dialogue among them. In one case, a panelist argued vehemently that because two others on stage were married, they should only be allowed 5 minutes each. After that heated disagreement was resolved somewhat unpleasantly, and in full view of the thousands in the audience, my next panel practically dissolved into a fistfight because one speaker had prepared a brief slide presentation and another speaker didn't like that she hadn't done the same. So she reached over to unplug the projector, and the guy slapped her hand away. I had to physically separate them. Certainly there was a history between them, but this was based on not just different personalities but also extremely different ideologies that they each found threatening.

It isn't much of a secret to realize that there isn't a whole lot of empirical evidence to support the notion that one model is significantly better than all others for *every* case. Although it is true that certain approaches or strategies are empirically supported for particular diagnostic entities, the validity of these studies can be called into question because the studies don't necessarily reflect the realities of how counseling actually takes place behind closed doors. Nevertheless, even when an assortment of counselors supposedly practice the same model, they may still be doing so in very different ways that reflect their own styles. Cognitive–behavioral counseling, as one example, is hardly a single, homogeneous entity, especially considering that Albert Ellis, Aaron Beck, Judith Beck, Michael Mahoney, Donald Meichenbaum, and others all have (and had) quite different personalities and styles. A few of them no longer even identify exclusively with that approach, having moved on to other ideas.

As mentioned previously, many within our profession are still debating the most basic assumptions that underlie counseling efforts: whether we should be directive or nondirective; promote insight or action; play the role of a coach, teacher, confidant, doctor, or collaborator; focus on feelings, thoughts, or behavior. They even debate the most legitimate time period on which to direct our attention: "You can't really resolve a core issue until you deal with unresolved issues from the past," "The most legitimate focus of counseling is *always* targeted on the present moment, what clients are experiencing in the here and now," "It is only when we plan for the future that we can truly make informed decisions and guide the trajectory of our lives."

It may appear that we only tend to quibble about whether counseling should be attuned to the past, present, or future, but this is just one area of disagreement. Members of our profession argue about whether it is best to deal with feelings versus thoughts versus behavior. They debate whether it is best to do individual, group, or family sessions. There are so many distinctly different (or maybe not so very different) schools of thought that each comes with its own proclamations, values, concepts, and rules. Several dominant ideologies hold their own conferences for their followers.

But what gets lost in all these debates about who has cornered truth is that it has become increasingly more difficult to locate our own singular voice and unique style among all the pressure to conform to the overlords of a cognitive behavior, emotionally focused, psychodynamic, narrative, feminist, or any other orientation. Each represents a tribe with its own culture and customs and a determination to establish itself as the dominant ideology.

Sorting Out Clanging Voices

Ryan Neace, a counselor who runs a clinic in an urban area, mentions how one of the most frustrating aspects of learning to be a counselor was dealing with all the powerful, conflicting opinions directed his way by supervisors, instructors, and authors. "There were these nearly incessant, clanging voices telling me that I had to do a whole bunch of foreign and complicated things to help people therapeutically—all of which I was pretty darn sure I didn't know how to do." Much of this resulted from the typical sort of training we all get in graduate school in which our instructors might impress on us the truth of a particular orientation or approach. Neace is quick to point out, however, that each of the masters developed models that best fit their own particular personalities, contexts, cultures, and client populations, which are not necessarily relevant to what any of us are doing today. "Half the time they were just making stuff up," Neace comments. "They were brilliant of course but making things up nonetheless."

If people tell you something for long enough, Neace believes, you start to internalize it, even think it is factual or truthful. The challenge for many of us occurs a few years later when we find ourselves struggling to help our own clients. "You sit in front of them and have to contend with all of those voices telling you how do to this or that helpful thing rather than leading with who you are." Then Neace mentions that when we add to the mix the voices from our parents, families, teachers, coaches, mentors, childhood traumas, "the internal chorus can boom so loud that we are unable to access ourselves at all—we are too busy trying to live up to someone else's ideal about the way things should work. Then we spend less time listening to the clients in front of us and experiencing who they are and what pain they are bearing."

Neace is even more blunt about the sorts of barriers this can present when we are trying to develop our own signature style of helping others: "There stands between us a mountain of bull crap, academic pretense, plus another heap of cultural factors related to things like race, age, socioeconomic class, gender, and sexual orientation, that also require our studied attention—plus our own pain and pathology. In other words, really connecting with clients, around, through, and in between all of this, is darn near impossible."

So what's the secret to cutting through all these influences and factors and this noise? Neace's secret is that he tries to lead himself and follow his client rather than some idea or theory to which he was previously attached. "While others might overly focus on a diagnostic entity, or looking for a father figure or attachment object, I tell myself that the most important thing is connecting with this person in the room. This means that sometimes I must tear down the walls erected by my education and licensure and certifications—all within the bounds of ethical and moral restraints. It means I acknowledge my privilege and share my power. It means I allow the permeable empathic membrane that exists between us to be pushed on, expanded, and ultimately pushed through. At times, it is even torn."

The consequence of such a therapeutic style is that at times we must strip ourselves down to our core. When we come face to face with our own cherished beliefs, when we discover our authentic voice, there are fewer places to hide. And there's nobody else to blame when things go wrong, as they inevitably will at times.

Going Beyond the Master

Jon Carlson, who was one of the most prominent Adlerian theorists throughout his career, found a way to reconcile his strong allegiance to Adler's theory and yet also develop his own voice influenced by so many other philosophies, ideas, and individuals. We collaborated on a dozen books together; most of them involved in-depth interviews with the greatest therapeutic minds of the past century. It would be impossible to listen to and interact with such charismatic, brilliant thinkers without internalizing some of what they were saying—and making it part of us.

Although Carlson had studied Adler's writing for 40 years, written many books and articles about the great man, edited the flagship journal, produced films about the theory, and taught at Adler University, he still admitted there was so much he didn't know and understand. "I knew I was a good therapist and could work with most anyone in any situation, yet I worked as myself, not as a disciple of Adler. Whenever I would do a live demonstration at a conference or workshop, I would frequently be asked by someone in the audience, 'Which Adlerian technique is that?' or 'Was what you did even Adlerian?' I would just shrug and admit I didn't know."

Carlson laughed, giving the subject some more thought, then added, "Finally, I began to respond to those questions by just saying that what I did was Adlerian enough for me." He explained that given that he lived in different times and contexts, his job was the same as that of any good student, which was to go beyond the master.

Barry Duncan, introduced in the previous chapter, believes strongly in the secret that to be truly effective using any strategy or intervention, the counselor must own it, must internalize and personalize it in such a way that it is authentic rather than just a rote application of something that was learned from others. "Who are we, really?" he asks. "Are we simply clones of our mentors and supervisors? The tradition in any professional guild is for apprentices to imitate their masters, do exactly what they do so they don't get in over our heads. Whether in carpentry or counseling, we are taught the proper way to look at a job and equipped with the skills and resources necessary to build a cabinet or prop up a fragile ego."

There is a danger in failing to truly internalize the voices of our teachers, supervisors, and mentors. At times, we hear their words come out of our mouths and sometimes even transform ourselves into an obedient mini-me who channels this role model down to the exact gesture and tone we are imitating. We spend our lives and careers following in the footsteps of others who have come before us. In many ways, we deify these authors, presenters, and notable figures, acting as if they were superheroes who are infallible and cut from a different cloth than we could ever be. At what other professional conferences do attendees line up to seek the autographs of luminaries in the field? Do forensic accounting or neuroimmunology conferences have participants hovering over the celebrities in attendance? I think it's nice and all that we give such attention and appreciation to leaders our profession, but I also think that counselors in the field are far better clinicians than some of those who are commanding all the attention.

The Secret to Developing a Signature Style of Practice

What is the secret to discovering (or creating) your own therapeutic style and counseling voice? In part, it is a function of experience and maturity: The more time we spend engaged in the work, especially *reflective* time, the more likely it is that our own values, beliefs, preferences, and interests seep into the sessions. The process begins with questioning and challenging the status quo: Why is it absolutely necessary to proceed in this way? What would happen if I did *this* instead? Those we admire the most, the inventors of new models or approaches, did just that—question why we've always done things a particular way and suggest, as well as test, possible alternatives that could be far more effective in certain situations.

Many of the authors of the most popular theories have talked about their own frustrations early in their careers. They found themselves limited by the approach that had then been at their disposal. In the beginning and the middle of the 20th century, almost all the major alternative models were developed by those practicing orthodox psychoanalysis. They found themselves questioning some of the basic propositions but still wished to hold onto the ideas that fit their needs as well as those of their clients. Thus, Carl Jung, Alfred Adler, Karen Horney—not to mention even Albert Ellis, Fritz Perls, and so many others—all shook off the bonds of attachment to orthodoxy in order to develop a unique, signature style that better reflected their beliefs and personalities.

Another important component involves truly knowing what's most important to you and your clients rather than simply a priority of someone else. This person may be bright and talented, even forward thinking, but that doesn't mean that what he or she has developed fits you perfectly without considerable adjustments. Some of us are loud, passionate, and charismatic, others are soft spoken and far more gentle in manner. Some counselors just love working in the realm of emotion and drama, whereas others prefer an atmosphere that is measured and controlled. Some enjoy the relative sanctity of a single person in the room, and other practitioners thrive on the chaos of working with large families or groups.

One of the norms within counseling for many decades has been that you aren't considered a legitimate practitioner unless you can clearly articulate which school of thought you belong to. As soon as you might mention a particular label—humanistic, psychodynamic, cognitive–behavioral, feminist, constructivist—you get a knowing look, as if that explains who you are and what you stand for, in the same way that people might ask, "So what's your sign? Aquarius? Oh, that explains it."

We need to eschew these simplistic labels and embrace the idea that one can subscribe to a particular theoretical framework as a home without necessarily following every prescription to the letter or behaving in lockstep with whatever is considered to be gospel. As mentioned previously, one would only have to watch an assortment of counselors following their espoused theory in practice to decide that they hardly resemble one another when in action. Some counselors are soft spoken, some rather dramatic and provocative. Some are in a hurry, and others take their time. Some specialize in bipolar disorder, others survivors of abuse, each of which may require a different kind of dosage.

What is increasingly clear is that the most important part of this discussion, the ultimate secret, is that you must feel comfortable in your counselor shoes, as if the method and style eventually feels natural to you, as if it is a part of you—which it is! The secret to finding your own unique voice is to value this task as an essential mission.

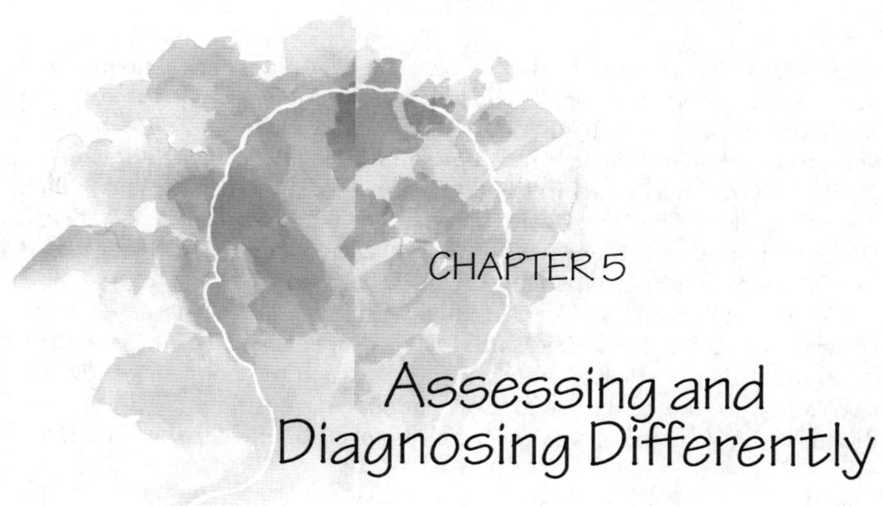

CHAPTER 5

Assessing and Diagnosing Differently

There are all kinds of ways in which counselors use diagnosis and assessment in their work. Our profession of counseling has been privileged, more than most others, to rely on systems from a variety of different disciplines in the social sciences, education, and human services. We are certainly fluent in the concepts and nomenclature of the *Diagnostic and Statistical Manual of Mental Disorders,* but we also rely on other systems that may emphasize developmental tasks and stages, systemic dynamics to better understand family functioning, even behavioral labeling that seeks to name situation-specific actions rather than pigeonholing a person's essence into a discrete category.

We assess all kinds of things in a variety of different ways. Take groups for instance. Imagine that you just asked members how they would like to respond to a fairly provocative statement by someone who said, "This whole group thing is a colossal waste of time." You scan the room and see some people shaking their heads, others looking down at their feet. But nobody will utter a word in response. Complete, total silence goes on for several minutes. So what do you do?

The answer depends very much on what the silence really means at that particular moment. Are members being resistant and obstructive? Are they confused? Perhaps they are flooded emotionally and just need time to sort out what they are feeling and what they want to say? In any case, the secret to dealing with silence begins with figuring out what the behavior is actually communicating, whether thoughtful reflection, bewilderment, resistance, or perhaps fear of saying or doing the wrong thing.

The choice regarding how to respond is contingent on all kinds of things that are assessed, such as what happened previously, norms within the group, the reading of nonverbal cues, and other contextual factors. If it is decided that members are confused, then further elaboration and explanation are indicated. If members appear resistant in some way, perhaps demonstrating their unwillingness to continue the discussion, then a different direction altogether must be considered, or at least a conversation must be had about members' reluctance. And if it is assessed that group members are simply reflecting on what was said, formulating what they want to say, then it's best to give them more time and wait the silence out.

"There is often a beauty in silence," counselor Liz Eddy explains when discussing one of her most valuable secrets. "If clients don't talk you can always explore with them what the silence means to them, what it was like for them. And perhaps why it was uncomfortable."

The secret for many exceptional counselors is to value assessment systems, consider the data gleaned from objective measures, consult a differential diagnostic decision tree, but then supplement those suggestions and hypotheses with a far more collaborative and relational process that more actively involves the client's own input and meaning making.

Collaborative Assessment

I want to mention a comment by Barry Duncan once again, as one of his primary missions has been to develop ways to reliably and easily measure outcomes as well as the strength of the relationship alliance. "This allows me to deal directly and transparently with clients, involving them in all decisions that affect their care and keeping their perspectives the centerpiece of everything I do. In addition, it serves as an early warning system that identifies clients who are not benefiting so that the client and I can chart a different course. I do everything I can to harvest, recruit, enlist, and utilize client resources, strengths, and resiliencies, to rally these unique client attributes to the cause of change."

This notion of collaborative assessment, rather than traditional ways that counselors might typically choose a diagnostic label, implies that meaningful understanding of a client's world and issues can hardly be reduced to a singular categorization. This oversimplification of complex and multidimensional phenomena may satisfy research protocols, insurance companies, and blank spaces on required forms but hardly best serves our clients or provides optimal guidance for creating and maintaining solid relationships.

Once we adopt a more collaborative approach to assessment, there are greater opportunities to delve more deeply into aspects of the client experience that are often more clinically useful:

- Exploring cultural and individual contexts for client behavior and experience
- Changing working diagnoses to more functional and useful conceptualizations
- Determining which client (and counselor) expectations are unrealistic or distorted
- Clarifying what has been working most and least effectively

Michael Hoyt, a brief therapy practitioner who has written a lot about functioning within the managed care system, has found that one of his assessment secrets begins with initial pattern recognition. He has developed a five-phase temporal structure in which we might consider assessment an evolving process. "The stages tend to be pyramidal or epigenetic," Hoyt explains. "That is, they tend to occur in sequence, and each flows from the preceding one so that successful work in one preconditions the next stage." This process begins of course when the client first makes a choice to seek help, and the first assessment decision is how best to create the optimal alliance for defining therapeutic goals and desired outcomes. Over time, assessment might focus on measuring goal attainment, how to prevent relapses, and the best follow-up plan. For Hoyt, this is the key to operating most efficiently, which is an important consideration for counselors who work in agencies or organizations in which they have limited time to make a difference.

Looking Backward to Move Forward

Although Jon Carlson acknowledged the realities of today's practice, in which brief counseling has become the norm and managed care has become the overarching, controlling authority, he lamented the lack of time and focus devoted to exploring a client's history in order to better understand the meaning of present issues and problems. Although it is certainly the case that it isn't absolutely necessary to secure a complete developmental family, cultural, medical, and social history in order to help someone, it is often useful to have at least broad strokes that may signal clues as to how and why problems may have developed—and may reoccur in the future.

As a passionate Adlerian theorist, Carlson was especially interested in clients' earliest recollections and their meaning. He developed and adapted over time a process in which clients were asked to remember something significant before the age of 8, a memory that could actually be seen with detail and feeling. He didn't explain the reasoning behind this but just found that this was an excellent way to keep the client talking and sharing, simultaneously creating a relational bond as well as collecting possibly important data. "Although such recollections are from the past," Carlson explained, "what we remember, and how we remember it, is very much in the present. People project their lifestyle and values into these stories. They actually end up describing what they are like today; how they see themselves, others, and the world; and how they must act today."

This strategy, one of Carlson's favorite and most useful secrets, ultimately helps clients to change some of their faulty beliefs, challenges some of their dysfunctional assumptions, and identifies those that are stopping them from reaching their articulated goals. He mentioned several case examples of meaningful recollections to illustrate the process:

> *Betty:* "I was 6 years old. I told my mom that I wanted to go fishing; she told my brother that he had to take me, he had to go and dig the worms and had to bait my hook. He did all the work and I caught the biggest fish but my brother baited my hook. I felt all good and happy."

Sasha: "I was about 6 or so. I remember waking up and going downstairs and no one was up. So I went to get some cereal and sat on the couch and waited for someone else to get up."

Brenda: "I had to walk to school. It was seven blocks from my house. One day, when I was in first grade, I slipped in a puddle and sat down in it and my seat was all wet. I didn't know what to do. There wasn't time to go home so I went to school and walked very carefully trying to make sure no one could see my backside. I worried all day that people would laugh at me and see that my pants were wet."

While exploring and analyzing the possible meanings of these recollections as part of his collaborative assessment process, Carlson noted that Betty initially appeared uncertain of her ability to care for herself. By contrast, Sasha's story possibly signaled relative independence. In Brenda's case, he mentioned the value of possibly exploring issues of shame and perhaps feeling that she had nobody to literally watch her back.

One need not be an Adlerian, or psychodynamically inclined, in order to probe family and social history. The secret that Carlson mentioned is not so much the technique of inviting early recollections as taking a position of curiosity and not-knowing in order to invite and empower clients to become more confident experts on their own experience.

Although assessment has often been framed and practiced within the context of distributing questionnaires, administering tests, conducting intake or mental status interviews, and applying standard diagnostic protocols, there are also many alternative ways that counselors favor particular observations they find revealing and useful. Carlson once again mentioned one of his favorites: the ways in which body art talks as a projective technique. After all, when someone takes the time, as well as invests resources and pain, to permanently advertise a particular message on his or her precious skin, it is difficult not to pay attention.

"Tattoos are clinical gold mines," Carlson shared. "Ink is everywhere these days and not just on soldiers, sailors, bikers, and prisoners. Sometimes tattoos are easy to spot; other times you have to directly ask clients if they have any." It was at this point that Carlson liked to ask them to tell the story behind each one. And even if they didn't have a tattoo, he would then follow up to ask, "If you did have a tat, what would that look like, what would you say, and where would you place it on your body?" Of those who had taken the plunge already, he would ask about any regrets or images they wished were removed. In his mind, Carlson found tattoos to be representational stories of meaningful experiences. As examples he referred to an Iraq War veteran who displayed on his arm "You don't know prayer until you know suffering" and a recently divorced woman in her 40s who had inscribed on her chest "Do what you love." She was now prepared to follow her own dreams instead of only supporting those of her ex-husband and children.

Carlson recalled a homeless man he had treated for alcohol and drug problems who had the words "Born to lose!" on his forearm. Carlson was curious about the message this man showed to the world and so asked him, "Don't you mean 'Born to win'?"

The man hesitated for a long moment, considering that alternative, then broke out into a huge grin. Then he said, "I thought there was something not quite right about that. Maybe I'll get it changed."

Beyond the messages that tattoos might carry as a personal statement, Carlson also found them revealing as a means of assessing other behavior that might not be immediately obvious. He was especially interested in research that indicated that certain risky behaviors, as well as possible drug and alcohol use, are associated with particular kinds of body art. "Some of them are clearly a statement of individuality, or a love of art, symbol, and story. But those of us who wonder should also remember that while a few are tattooed for shock value, many of our clients are just using their bodies to tell us stories, to share emotions. They're wearing their pain, their loss, their hopes, their values, their dreams, and fantasies. No small number of people (especially our clients) are using the ink to try to remake themselves; to paint over the memories, struggles, or perceived inadequacies that plague them; and to thereby redesign their image in a way more to their own liking."

Assessing Strengths and Resources

It's no longer much of a secret that for far too long members of our profession (and especially our colleagues in other mental health disciplines) have been obsessed with and overly focused on what's wrong with people and have failed to balance attention on psychopathology, problems, disorders, and mental illness with at least equal attention on strengths, resources, resilience, and looking for exceptions to the problems. The movements launched by positive psychology, solution-focused counseling, and posttraumatic growth have reminded us how important it is to assess sources of support rather than exclusively collecting data on disturbing symptomatology.

I learned this lesson long ago with one particular client who was suffering from debilitating physical pain, discomfort, and disabilities associated with a chronic neurological disease. Each week she would take up most of the session describing all of her various and latest maladies. Her extremities felt numb. Her vision was blurred. She frequently lost her balance. She felt sudden, crippling pain throughout her arms and legs. And then there were all the side effects from her various medications—loss of bladder control, lack of libido, weight gain—plus the collateral emotional volatility, which included arguing with her husband, being short tempered, having depression, having a fear of dying and fear of living, and the list went on and on. Furthermore, she was perfectly entitled to complain, given the overwhelming assortment of misery that she was experiencing on a daily basis.

This was long before many of the new movements mentioned above were invented, so I was bumbling along the best I could, trying to listen and support her. In truth, however, it was so incredibly discouraging and depressing for me to just sit and listen to her complain every hour. I felt helpless and at times bored, as our time together was so predictable. I learned to avoid asking the questions "So how are you doing this week?" or "What's new?" because I realized what would follow would be a long list of miserable complaints about not only her deteriorating physical condition but also how nobody in her life wanted to listen to her anymore. Guiltily I admitted to myself that I felt the same way. I was losing my compassion and empathy for her because I felt so burdened by problems I could do nothing to fix. I would tell myself that it was enough to just listen and "hold" her, but I suppose I didn't really believe that.

One day our session was more difficult than usual. My client had been going on, nonstop, for the whole hour—actually we were *past* the time limit but I couldn't get a word in to slow her down. It had been a particularly trying week for her, so she recited so many new maladies and symptoms that were bothersome, none of which I could do anything about. And any time I tried to refocus our attention on her attitude or coping strategies, she'd ignore me and just keep going. It was more out of desperation than anything else that I finally and firmly interrupted her.

"Look, I'm so, so sorry that it was just a difficult week for you. And I realize we are out of time."

She gave me a sad, dispirited look, as if I too were rejecting her like everyone else.

"Before you go," I continued as gently as possible, "I wonder if you could share with me just one good thing that happened this week? What's one nice thing that happened or one experience you had that, if not pleasurable, was at least satisfying?"

She just looked at me, crossed her arms, and remained silent.

I guess one of the most important secrets I learned previously was not to ask people to do things that they weren't willing or capable (yet) of doing. I realized in that moment that even though I was requesting a very simple task, one she could surely complete if she wanted to, it was obvious that I was breaking our pattern. She needed to use our time together to complain because she wasn't allowed to do that anywhere else. But I also realized that there were limits to how therapeutic this was becoming for her, using our sessions exclusively to focus on the misery of her life. Or perhaps if I were more honest, I'd admit that I was tired of feeling so helpless and worthless being with her.

"Just before you go today," I tried one more time, "could you just humor me and tell me one thing that happened that made you smile this week, or laugh, or maybe a time when even for a few minutes you forgot you had this horrible disease?"

Still a blank look.

"Okay," I said, holding out my hands. "I get it. But how about next time we are together, we save the last 5 minutes for you to report only on a few things, or even one thing, that went reasonably well, or something you are proud of, or maybe just one time that, in spite of your pain and discomfort, you were still able to accomplish something important to you." Just to make sure that she could comply with this rather simple task, I instructed her to make a list throughout the week of *anything* that made her smile or feel some semblance of satisfaction, if not joy.

The battle between us continued over a few months because it really took her that long to learn how to talk about herself and her life in more positive ways, even for a few minutes. I don't know for certain how much this helped her because she still seemed to find the greatest relief in telling me about what was wrong rather than anything that felt right. Maybe she was just humoring me during those few minutes at the end of each subsequent session. But I did learn a secret from our interactions: that no matter how miserable and hopeless someone feels, it is really, really important to help him or her assess the strengths and positive things going on as well. I know this seems somewhat obvious now that strengths-based approaches are taking hold, but I still find I must keep reminding myself to balance problems with successes, given that I'd been trained for so many years to only assess negative symptoms.

Echoing this perspective, Miguel Gallardo, a psychologist who specializes in advocacy work within the Latino community as well as with other monolingual cultural groups, wonders, "What would happen if we saw everyone for what strengths and resources they bring with them versus what is wrong with them? What would counseling look like if we did not have to worry so much about making sure that we were always adhering to narrowly defined ways of practicing or self-protecting our professional livelihood over serving others first and foremost?"

Gallardo is quick to point out that he is not advocating unethical behavior or encouraging counselors to do whatever they want, rather he is emphasizing that there is a point at which we are so concerned with technical procedures that we lose our own humanity. "Our current mental health delivery systems continue to perpetuate performance over people. Quantity over quality. Why can't we measure our success and outcomes with the voices of the people we serve over numbers? We have become so seduced with bells and whistles, and with smoking mirrors, that we have forgotten the humanity and the humility in our work and what we do."

Gallardo spends much of his professional life teaching and supervising other counselors who work in underserved communities, and he doesn't believe that many of our existing approaches are adapted and well suited for these populations. "I do not have any secrets, but believe we need to revisit, reassess, and reopen our once noted but long forgotten foundations as human beings. We are relational; we need to be loved, express love, and disseminate love in all that we do. We have never been more connected as human beings while simultaneously being more disconnected than we have ever been. Our mantra in the counseling professions should be people over policies, procedures, and performance."

And *Then* What Happened?

As careful and systematic as we might be doing initial assessments, such actions tend to dissipate over time once things get going. The problems or initial concerns are hopefully resolved. Clients say goodbye and go on their way. The case is closed, and we move on to the next ones.

We have all been admonished multiple times that our jobs don't necessarily end when clients walk out the door. As we well know, relapses are not only commonplace but usually expected. The truth of the matter is that many changes don't last, especially without ongoing support. There are many different reasons for this, the first of which is that there are considerable benefits to backsliding and remaining mired in the status quo:

1. Attention and sympathy from others
2. Externalized blame for everything that goes wrong
3. Avoidance of ongoing responsibility for negative outcomes
4. Ready excuses for behaving badly—and getting away with it
5. Being able to control one's misery on one's own terms
6. Distraction from other issues that may be far more threatening
7. Avoidance of the unknown

If that helps explain the payoffs or helpful consequences of failing to continue making progress, there are other reasons why changes that occur in counseling—or in everyday life—are not often maintained. Much depends on personal factors within clients, such as their levels of resilience, hardiness, motivation, impulsivity, emotional volatility, and tolerance for pain and discomfort, and especially how well we have prepared them for setbacks and relapses. Internalized attitudes play a huge part as well, the self-talk clients rely on when things don't go their way. We are well aware that no matter how much progress was made during sessions and how dramatic the results, certain cognitive patterns will sabotage the possibility that changes stick over time: "Maybe this isn't as important as I thought it was. Besides, it's too much work and takes too much time."

Most of the time, we never hear from our clients again; we just assume that's good news. They are cured and don't need us anymore. They've moved on to better, or at least different, things. There's also the possibility that they've gone back to old patterns and feel too ashamed to admit it. Regardless of the long-term outcome, usually we don't ever find out. Perhaps I should say that differently: We don't make a concerted effort to follow up with them.

We have good excuses for our failure to systematically follow up with our clients after sessions end. We don't wish to intrude or bother them, assuming that if they really needed us again, they'd call. We are also so overwhelmed much of the time just trying to keep up with the current caseload and work and family responsibilities that there are precious few opportunities to check in with people from the past. Ultimately I suppose the most legitimate reason is that we may see it as the client's responsibility to ask for help when it's needed.

Some Essential Assessment Questions

Before we leave the topic of assessment and move on to the sort of deep listening that often reveals more than any structured questions we might pose to clients, I'd like to summarize what I consider some crucial areas to consider. These are questions that are designed to sort out what may be going on and yet not foreclose on other more complex, multifaceted dimensions of what has been presented—and what may have been left out. After all, we sometimes get in trouble when we make assumptions based on prior experience that are not necessarily applicable with a particular individual.

1. What is the client's *story?* Every client has a story to tell that goes beyond a presentation of problems and recitation of symptoms. This is the narrative in which the client casts himself or herself in the role of hero, villain, or helpless bystander. The tales may initially lack coherence, but over time we come to understand them as a series of weekly installments that may be best categorized as a drama, thriller, disaster, soap opera, situation comedy, or sometimes even game show.
2. What is the client's *experience?* Beyond the story that is being told, how is the client metabolizing the events that have been described? This involves not only coping ability but also the lived experience in a multitude of other ways.
3. What does the client *believe* is going on? It is crucial to identify and understand the client's perceptions and conceptualizations of the presenting problem. Even though it is highly unlikely that we would agree with this self-defeating and self-limiting assessment, clients tend to fire us and not come back if they don't think we are listening to and honoring their viewpoints.
4. What *seems* to be happening? Of course we can never really know for certain what is really happening in any client's life. But it helps to modestly and cautiously generate some tentative hypotheses that may or may not be revised and updated as we learn more.
5. What is the consensual name for this? Diagnostic systems are convenient placeholders for things we don't yet understand. Once we assign a name to something it seems to reduce uncertainty and anxiety, whether the name is accurate or not in truly holding the essence of the phenomenon. I've always been struck during nature tours how the guides always insist on providing the names of every plant, animal, insect, and object that is seen, as if that captures the most important part of the experience.
6. What *else* could it be? This is a tough one, because once we settle on a diagnosis or name for something, it's hard to surrender it to something else, even in the face of compelling evidence. This is why one of my secrets has always been to embrace my uncertainty and doubt about almost anything; such tentativeness, if we can live with it, often leads to amazing new discoveries.

7. What has the client already tried? It is standard operating procedure to collect from clients the most comprehensive list of strategies, options, and behaviors they have already found fruitless. I love, for instance, to ask specifically what clients liked most and least about any previous counseling experiences they have had. In a sense, they will tell us directly what most annoys them.
8. What has been working so far? Likewise, it is always helpful to identify anything that has previously proven useful. This is often tough going, as clients tend to like to focus on their complaints and troubles and are often reluctant to look at exceptions, minor victories, and triumphs.
9. What strategy or approach *might* work best? It's the *might* that is most important in this question because there's no way we can possibly know what will work for sure. I find this question most reassuring because it reminds me that all of counseling is an experiment, a testing of hypotheses, a series of adaptations and recalibrations in light of new evidence and new installments in the stories that unfold.

The secret of any solid assessment process is not just to value reliability and consistency in the ways in which we collect information so as to standardize our procedures in order to make normative comparisons. It is also important to use different methods depending on the issues. We hone in on particular features or sources of data depending on what might best guide our therapeutic actions. For some clients it is imperative that we collect a comprehensive and complete medical history; for others it may be more important to explore family-of-origin issues, or characteristic defense mechanisms, or interpersonal patterns, or even in some cases more specific data that are directly relevant to the case. As I'll mention repeatedly, one of the most important secrets of exceptional counselors is their willingness to continuously adapt what they do, and how they do it, to better customize and operationalize their strategies.

CHAPTER 6

Deep, Deep Listening

There's listening. And then there's really, really *listening*. Call it what you like, but this type of intense, devoted, complete engagement in a conversation is what Theodore Reik referred to as "listening with the third ear." He meant that our goal is not just to hear the other with hovering attention but also to listen to the voice inside us, the one that occasionally offers bits of intuitive wisdom.

Why else would anyone bother to ever consult with us if we can't hear, see, notice, and discover things that others might miss or fail to respond to? It isn't just our training and experience that allows us to recognize the underlying, subtle messages that people often communicate: It's our *willingness* to do so. The truth of the matter is that it's such hard work, and demands such a high degree of commitment and focus, to truly listen to someone with *all* of one's capacity, that about the only place this ever seems to happen is within counseling relationships. Where else do we resist the impulse to answer the phone, respond to a text—prohibit interruptions of any sort? Where else do two (or more) people face one another in close proximity, insulated from any outside distractions or influences, and then agree to only speak about the most important issues of life?

The reality of course is that deep listening is an ideal to which we strive but achieve only sporadically. It often depends on the client, the issues on the table, but also whatever is going on in our own lives. There are some cases in which we are so riveted that time flies by as if the conversation were only a few minutes; then there are other sessions that seem to last for hours, and when we glance at the clock we can see that the hands have hardly advanced at all.

Love Is a Four-Letter Word

Love is one of those words with a *lot* of different meanings that can easily be misconstrued. That is one reason the term is consistently avoided in any discussion of what happens in counseling, especially with some of the dangers of exploitation or sexual improprieties. Yet although we talk about romantic love, platonic love, and parental love, the Greeks referred to *agape* as the type of unyielding, compassionate, unconditional love, respect, and affection offered to someone, even with one's flaws and annoyances. It always involves some form of sacrifice because it means placing someone else's interests before our own. Thus, it takes a certain ability and willingness (and often payment for the effort) to love someone who sometimes works so hard to be unlovable.

One of our jobs is to help clients to love themselves once again, and we often do that by demonstrating our own deep caring and deep listening, communicating consistently to others that what they have to say is indeed important and worth listening to. In the best sense, we don't switch on a technique but rather feel a passionate interest in the conversation. One counselor remarks, "This deep listening represents a true yearning to know the other person's story and understand the intricacies of the other person's life. The counselor's stance here is similar to reading a treasured book, watching a cliffhanger of a television show, or showing up early for a movie that you have been anticipating for months. There is a passion and excitement to know, to understand the other." She concludes by suggesting that "counseling is most successful when a counselor offers two things to his or her clients. These two things are love and understanding. The love is a nonromantic, nonpossessive love. This is an expression of caring for the person as a valuable and unique individual with the same joy, pain, and varied experiences we each have."

Here's an example of how deep listening can magnify our helping efforts. Barry Duncan is known primarily as an empirical researcher even though he uses poetic language to describe the almost ethereal aspects of the relational connection. He mentions one of his clients, Tina, who was young, poor, disenfranchised, heavily medicated, repeatedly hospitalized, and bestowed at age 22 with the label of chronic schizophrenic. Duncan describes her with short, cropped hair and a pixie-like demeanor. He greeted her in his most professional manner.

"Before I could even sit down," Duncan recalls, "Tina started to take off her clothes and started mumbling to herself. I just stared in disbelief, in total shock really. Tina was undaunted by my dismay and quickly was down to her bra and underwear when I finally broke my silence, hearing laughter in the distance, and said, 'Tina, what are you doing?'"

Duncan was disheartened to see that Tina responded not with words at all but rather with continued action, this time removing her bra as if it had become suddenly uncomfortable. "So there we were, a graduate student, speechless, in his first professional encounter, and a client sitting nearly naked, mumbling quite loudly but still nothing I could understand."

Duncan watched her standing there, now horrified that she seemed to be contemplating taking off her underwear next. Finally, in desperation, he awoke from the shock of his temporary stupor and pleaded, "Tina, would you please do me a big favor? I mean, I would really appreciate it."

Tina looked up and met Duncan's eyes for the first time. She looked confused but remained mute, just staring at him.

"Look," he pleaded, "I'd really appreciate it if you would put your clothes back on and help me get through this initial interview." Duncan mentioned that he'd done these sorts of intake assessments previously, but never with someone who had unceremoniously stripped naked. "To tell you the truth, Tina, you are freaking me out. Would you mind getting dressed?"

Tina shrugged and whispered in a quiet compliant voice, "Sure."

Duncan was so relieved and appreciative of her cooperation that he disclosed to her how much this helped him get through this assessment interview, about which he'd already been feeling apprehensive.

Immediately Tina broke out in a huge grin, almost as if nobody had ever thanked her before for being helpful. Duncan says, "I wound up getting to know Tina pretty well and often reminded her how she had helped me. The more I got to know Tina and realized that her actions, stemming from horrific abuse, were attempts to take control of situations in which she felt powerless, the angrier I became about her being used as a rite of passage for the psychology trainees—a practice that I stopped."

Duncan will never forget the secret he learned from Tina during that first meeting: "Authenticity matters. Whenever you feel in doubt, or uncertain, or confused, ask the client for help because you are both in this together."

Listen to What Is Not Being Said—and Other Subtleties

One consequence of getting into the zone of deep listening is that we are able to expand awareness to aspects of a client's experience that would not otherwise be recognizable, much less accessible. After all, every gesture, every action, every movement speaks about what a client is thinking, feeling, experiencing.

A new client enters the office and hands the counselor the intake forms that were distributed when he first checked in with the receptionist. The counselor briefly glances through the papers and then invites the client to have a seat. The client slowly shuffles over to a chair and almost collapses into the seat. They both just stare at each other for a few long minutes, each waiting for the other to break the silence. This is not a game the counselor is playing; rather, he is curiously processing all that he is taking in.

"You look like you've given up," the counselor finally says.

"Excuse me?"

"I said that you seem to have just given up."

"I don't know what you mean."

The counselor holds out the intake papers. "I see that you filled out the first page but then just gave up and didn't complete the rest. I'm wondering if that may be how you are dealing with things in life—making a token, minimum effort and then just giving up."

The client seems taken aback. "How could you know something like that about me? We just met and I haven't told you anything about me yet."

"Oh, I've been listening alright, just to some things other than what you have yet to reveal. It seems pretty clear to me that you don't want to be here. When you walked in you reminded me of someone who was about to occupy a jail cell for punishment."

There could be all kinds of other interpretations. Perhaps the client is communicating that he's special and doesn't have to follow the usual rules. Or maybe that he just doesn't understand what is expected. He could have simply not slept well the night before and now is out of sorts and confused. But regardless, the counselor relies on far more than the words that are said and listens deeply to other aspects of behavior that could be meaningful and significant. This isn't exactly much of a secret to most of us, but it does signify how important it is that we listen to the most subtle, hidden, and disguised nuances of a client's actions (or nonactions).

The interesting thing is that this challenge can become even more difficult for experienced counselors because it is so easy to become complacent and operate on autopilot, especially for those who think they've heard it all before.

Being Fully Present

There's really no secret at all to what it means to be fully engaged with someone in a relationship: It's about commitment and devotion. And let's face it—sometimes we are lazy, or we become bored, or we can't seem to get outside of ourselves. Sometimes we become so consumed with what we want to do next or how we might make sense of what is happening in the moment that we lose the ability to focus on remaining fully present in the moment.

Counselors are known to try all sorts of little tricks when they catch themselves leaving the room, so to speak, lapsing into fantasy or losing threads of the conversation. Deep breathing helps. So does simply reminding yourself to stay present every time you drift or wander.

Counselors who have studied Buddhist philosophy or practiced meditation or mindfulness on a daily basis have learned to hone their ability to remain attentive. Even more important, when they notice any internal chattering or external distractions they concentrate even harder to put aside everything else except what is happening right now.

Whereas mindfulness generally just refers to the greater awareness that attention has wandered, meditation represents a whole class of ways in which counselors have trained themselves to quiet their minds so that they can devote full and hovering attention to whatever is going on.

"Call me restless or lazy," one counselor admits, "but I've tried meditation and it just doesn't work for me." He confesses that he always begins his latest attempt with the best of intentions, but he just gets easily distracted, admitting maybe that's why he needs practice more than ever. "I know that these days everyone is into yoga, meditation, and mindfulness—yeah, even mindfulness-based counseling approaches—but that has just never worked for me."

Instead, this counselor prefers the type of mindfulness that comes from movement rather than stillness. "Throughout my life the way I've been able to turn off my brain and pay better attention to the here and now is through running or cycling or some other form of vigorous exercise. I've found that the secret to staying on course is never allowing myself the option to negotiate this time. I know that some people just routinely meditate every morning, just like brushing their teeth. It is the same with me and exercise. And that's taught me a lot about how to remain in the moment."

This counselor mentions a study he once read about world-class athletes, especially marathon runners, who, rather than trying to distract themselves or escape the excruciating suffering during a race with their heart rate hovering above 180, instead carefully and systematically monitor everything going on in their body. Breathing steady: check. Cramp starting in left calf: check. Gait balanced and steady: check. Each part of one's body is closely scrutinized for the slightest irregularity. And similar to how a Buddhist might talk about suffering as no different from any other sensation, the champion athlete uses mindfulness to embrace the pain rather than disown it.

As counselors we often function in similar ways, systematically tuning in to whatever thoughts, feelings, images, or ideas float through our heads, gently placing them aside as we accelerate attention and interest to the person(s) sitting before us. Discomforts, apprehensions, confusion all provide valuable input that is at once potentially distracting and revealing.

Such mind-disciplined laser focus is directed, as well, to all the things we observe, sense, feel, and hear in the room. Once we have entered that space of heightened awareness, we are readily able to see things that might otherwise remain invisible. We hear cues in speech and nonverbal tells that uncover nuances that previously seemed inscrutable. We are able to access intuitive resources that have been blinded. And we are able to engage in a kind of hyper-relational intimacy that would not have been possible without this kind of almost miraculous engagement.

Jose Cervantes mentions that his most valuable secret when working within indigenous and Latino/a communities is directly related to the way he has internalized a spiritually driven perspective that allows him to clear the emotional energy that he brings to sessions. He relies on a mindfulness-based perspective to develop the kind of presence that includes the unspoken visual, auditory, sensory, and emotional experiences from clients. "I'm interested in exploring the layers of human energy that are available and can inform and complement the verbal dialogue. I listen for images, for thoughts and feeling states, that I consider useful clues to decipher. It becomes a kind of 'metaphorical dialogue' that opens new windows to a client's identity and struggles."

Mindfulness: The Gift That Keeps on Giving

One of the secrets reported by a number of counselors is how the regular practice of mindfulness meditation has really helped them to maintain their attentiveness and ability to keep themselves focused on the moment. I'm not the best example of this. Every few years I make a promise to myself to begin a new commitment to meditation practice. I watch videos to inspire me. I listen to audio recordings, download meditation apps on my phone. I've even worn a string bracelet that was blessed by the Dalai Lama to remind me of my intention (it fell apart in the shower, as did my motivation to continue). With that confession, it occurs to me that each of us discovers our own unique path to becoming more centered and mindful, whether following formal meditation or perhaps other means of achieving some level of serenity, whether through exercise, walking, music (playing or listening), or a dozen other pathways. Regardless of the chosen method, most of us are certainly well aware of the benefits of mindfulness, which have been supported by considerable research: less anxiety and depression, better sleep, increased self-discipline, avoidance of substance abuse, improved compassion and empathy, and so on. Then there's the imperative that we are supposed to be practicing exactly those behaviors that we consider so advantageous for others (more on that later). After all, it's hard to teach someone something that we can't or won't do ourselves.

"For me," one counselor shares, "it is about breathing. My secret is that any time I catch myself (and I have to catch myself) losing the thread of the conversation, becoming bored or distracted, feeling anxious or concerned, triggered by something the client said, I try to remember to just breathe through it. The client would hardly notice anything different. I just close my eyes for a brief moment and take a minute to breathe deeply through my diaphragm, and on the outbreath my mantra that I repeat is 'Be here now.' It just reminds me to let go of whatever is on my mind and stay focused."

Jon Carlson tried hard to do this in almost every aspect of his life beyond counseling sessions. The process began for him, as it does with the counselor above, with a deep breath. "I start to focus on my breathing in order, first, to clear a picture of myself. It's as if I'm sitting across from myself, watching, observing, relaxing. Then I tell myself, almost as a silent prayer, may I be peaceful, satisfied, happy, safe, and free of suffering."

This last piece, the suffering, was a bit of a challenge for Carlson considering that he was fighting for his life in the hospital after barely surviving an experimental treatment for a rare form of cancer. Even though his precarious health was declining and he only had a few weeks left to live, his devotion to a lifetime of mindfulness and meditation practice served him well to keep an upbeat attitude and to reduce his complaints about pain and discomfort.

The next step, after practicing self-compassion, is to spread the feelings of well-being to others. Carlson explained, "I try hard, as often as I can, to picture my loved ones, my family, my students, colleagues, friends, and clients, and to imagine each one of them sitting in front of me. I wish each of them an existence free from suffering." What he meant by this was not simply an absence of discomfort, disappointment, rejection, and hurt but rather a mindful way of experiencing these potentially uncomfortable outcomes and embracing the lessons that can be learned. Yes, this seems ridiculously charming. But that's why monks and devotees spend their whole lives trying to attain something close to nirvana. It's also why most people rely on chemical shortcuts to reclaim a sense of peace and tranquility.

It is precisely this deep listening to oneself that allows us to go with the flow of what is unfolding in session (or in life). It counteracts our natural (or trained) habit of analyzing and ov无为nking everything. This is what has been described by the Chinese as (*wu wei*), or "effortless action." This becomes a state of harmony with the client in which conversation and interaction become less rehearsed and more natural and uncontrived. When we find ourselves in such a condition, we simply invite the client to take a seat, take a breath, and begin.

Deep Listening Has Never Been More Important

It is the reality of our contemporary lives that undivided attention is virtually extinct. Hardly anyone gives anyone else their full and complete presence anymore. Mobile devices and distractions have become so ubiquitous that nobody seems to care very much whether anyone else is really listening to them or not.

I had just completed a workshop on the primacy of the relationship in any helping effort. I had showed hilarious slides of six people sitting around a table, all on their phones with someone else, and everyone laughed appreciatively. I showed another slide of a guy sitting on the deck of his yacht, so engrossed in texting someone on his phone that he didn't notice a whale that had breached not 5 feet from his spot. Again the audience laughed, after which I made the point that counselors, more than most others, should be models of devoted presence in the moment. We should be willing and able to give full attention and deep listening to whomever we are with, regardless of the time and place. After all, we are supposed to teach others not just by lecturing and admonishing them but by demonstrating such behavior in our daily lives. This was a particularly impassioned speech because I feel so strongly about this. Not wanting to appear a hypocrite, I purposely leave my phone at home when I go out with friends or family. When I mentioned this, I saw a bunch of heads nodding in agreement.

We took a lunch break and I sat at a round table with five of the participants. Each and every one of them whipped out their phones, even before scanning the menu, and proceeded to spend much of our time together texting, e-mailing, or calling others. In other words, this behavior is so impervious to change, even when people are aware of the negative consequences, that I've decided I might as well accept that this is our new reality.

It would appear that, more than anything else, deep listening is going to be a lost art. People will no longer expect, much less demand, that others pay close attention to what they are saying without any other distractions. This means that (hopefully) one of the last sanctuaries of truly attentive behavior is within a counseling session. If we do nothing else, we communicate to our clients that they have our total and complete attention. And I believe this is becoming so increasingly rare, it is often healing in and of itself.

CHAPTER 7

Don't Forget the Context and Culture

"I'm not going to be able to continue my education," the girl announced to me. Then she looked away and started sobbing.

"Wait a minute. What do you mean?" I was dumbfounded. Aarshi was among the best and brightest girls in our scholarship program, one of several hundred girls in Nepal who had been at risk for being forced into early marriage or even sex slavery. Her parents sold vegetables on the street in Kathmandu, and she was the first girl in her family ever to attend secondary school. She had aspirations of going to medical school and becoming a surgeon some day.

Aarshi just looked down and started sobbing.

I waited. And waited. But there was no sign she would stop crying any time soon, so I prompted her to tell me what had happened. She had done well on her entrance exams for higher education and was in the top of her school academically. In addition, she had already been promised that our foundation would cover all of her expenses and provide a full scholarship. I couldn't imagine what sort of problem at this point could possibly change her mind.

"It's my father."

"Your father," I repeated.

She just nodded.

"What *about* your father?"

"He said I can't go to school anymore. He said school is for boys, not girls. He said I must work with my family to sell the vegetables. And it is not my place to question him."

"Of *course* you must question him!" I blurted out loud before I could stop myself. "This isn't fair after all your hard work. He *knew* what you were working toward. You said your family was so proud of what you were planning to do. You said . . ."

Aarshi shook her head and the tears started flowing again. "No," she finally said in a whisper. "You don't understand. I can't go against my father's wishes. I must do as he says."

It was my ignorance of the local customs and culture that led me to view this girl's predicament as I would have back home. I felt my own rage at the injustice of the ways in which girls and women were often treated in parts of the world. I had been trying to do something about that for some time but would often find myself in trouble because I failed to respect the local norms and try to work within them—at least a little. But I fancied myself a rebel and I lost perspective. I kept pushing Aarshi to ignore what her father told her, that he just didn't understand and appreciate how brilliant and capable she was, that she could do so much more than sell vegetables on the street. In addition, I was terrified that once she was pulled out of school she would be ripe for exploitation by an unscrupulous predator who promised her a job in India. Each year more than 10,000 Nepali girls are smuggled over the border to end up in brothels as sex slaves. I feared Aarshi would be next.

This is just one of so many examples of a do-gooder, well-intended counselor trying to do the right thing, or at least what seems right from the professional's own worldview, and doing harm because of ignorance and insensitivity. In this case, we were able to negotiate a compromise in which Aarshi was permitted to complete her secondary school education and perhaps, some time in the future, might be allowed to continue her education—perhaps not as a doctor ("That is for men, not girls") but maybe to train as a nurse. I suppose it is fairly obvious that this broke my heart.

A Reconceptualization of What Culture Means

If you think you are about to read the standard boilerplate statement and scolding about the critical importance of multiculturalism, diversity, advocacy, and support for the dispossessed, you are mistaken. I consider culture to be something far more broad and expansive than just one's ethnicity, race, religion, gender, socioeconomic status, native language, or sexual orientation. Although all these features are certainly core components of a client's experience, they do not necessarily capture the multidimensional aspects of identity. One secret is that culture is far more diverse and individualized than we usually acknowledge, encompassing not only physical features but one's interests, values, activities, geographical location, family structure, profession or job, and a hundred (or thousand) other possibilities.

A guy shows up in your office. He doesn't actually walk in but rolls in with his wheelchair. Immediately your diagnostic acumen leads you to assess that he is a voting member of the paraplegic constituency. You also notice that his arms are *huge*, signaling that he is likely some kind of athlete, and you soon learn that he plays wheelchair rugby and even aims to try out for the national Paralympic team. In just a few minutes, you learn more than you ever cared to know about the culture of this sport and what it means for him to be part of that team.

Before formulating too many assumptions about this client's issues, concerns, and background, you also learn that although he has relocated to the West Coast, he is originally from a small town in Texas. You can readily tell that he has some facial features that appear Asian or perhaps Middle Eastern. Sure enough, he tells you that his father is Muslim from India and his mother is Vietnamese. In addition, he grew up in a place where he was virtually the only minority child in his school other than members of the predominantly Mexican American community. It is interesting that although he tells you he doesn't understand a word of Hindi or Vietnamese, he learned to speak Spanish fluently from his friends.

Disabled: check. Biracial: check. An athlete: check. Bilingual: check.

Yet there is so much more.

It turns out that when asked the rather ambiguous prompt, "So tell me about the cultures that are most important to you," the man initially just shrugs, not to avoid the question but rather to give himself time to formulate a thorough and accurate response. Finally, after a lengthy pause, he smiles and says, "I'm an Aggie."

It turns out that when he is asked directly how he identifies himself culturally, the first thing that comes to mind for him is *none* of the characteristics previously mentioned. Because his family were immigrants, and he first arrived in the country as an adolescent, he grew up being told by his teachers that he'd end up working in the fields like everyone else in town. He remembers that before he could even speak proper English, he watched college football games. Although the big universities were hundreds of miles away from where he lived, he always dreamed that one day he might somehow attend higher education. Trapped in his wheelchair, he also dreamed that one day he'd play football for Texas A&M. Although he realized that his fantasy was hardly realistic, he became determined to follow through on his university pursuit, becoming the first one in his family to graduate. So when he is asked about his dominant cultural identity, the first thing that comes to mind is his pride as an alumnus. As if to emphasize this point, he shows you his ring with the crest of the university.

The point of this example, obviously, is that we should be careful to rein in our own assumptions about what cultural identity means to our clients. Just because someone has brown skin; or speaks Mandarin; or is almost 7 feet tall; or is a Republican, or an accountant, or a phillumenist (someone who collects matchboxes) doesn't mean that we have the slightest idea who they really are. Likewise, throwing someone into a cultural box because of some singular characteristic risks setting up a different kind overgeneralization, if not misguided prejudice. Just because someone is Bangladeshi American or Catholic or transgender or Mississippian doesn't mean we truly understand the context of his or her life until we dive much more deeply into all the different ways this person defines himself or herself and identifies with particular groups, interests, or labels.

Cultural Constructions

"Hey, I'm not here to fill out forms. I thought I was going to get counseling and not paperwork." The nicely dressed 45-year-old man was standing in front of the receptionist's desk looking very unhappy.

"I know," the receptionist answered with a smile meant to diffuse the man's frustration. "Nobody likes these forms but it actually saves you a lot of time by providing information that helps us to better serve you."

"But I just want to talk to someone. The counselor must already know who I am," he said almost apologetically. "I've been in the news a lot lately."

The receptionist looked puzzled, scrutinizing the man more closely but without visible recognition. "Well, I'm sure he is familiar with your case, but it's just a formality and you can't really get started until you fill these out." She pointed at the forms and then resumed whatever she had been working on before the interruption.

The counselor was within earshot of this conversation and so couldn't help but already form a diagnostic impression of this client heavily weighted in the narcissistic direction. But then he remembered a conversation he had been having earlier with a friend in which they were both complaining about the policies of medical offices asking them to fill out "stupid, tedious forms" that only repeat the same questions the doctor will ask anyway, as if he or she never bothered to look at the file. They had both decided that if you were considered important enough you could skip this form completion stage altogether. "Do they make the president fill out these stupid things?" he had wondered aloud.

It is context that determines whether we perceive someone as normal or pathological. One factor in whether you are viewed as crazy or eccentric is how much money you have. You can wash your hands a dozen times each day, lock yourself up inside, demand glass jars of only orange M&Ms, walk around shoeless, scream at others whenever you want, demand that you be treated as a godling, and if you are rich or famous you can get away with it and the behavior is excused as just unconventional. But if you happen to be one of the masses, you are at serious risk for being labeled mentally unbalanced. It's all about context.

Certainly cultural constructions, the media, and social norms are largely responsible for creating and enforcing what is considered acceptable—or even tolerable—behavior. But we counselors as well bring our own expectations into the mix, influencing the particular ways in which we assess and treat clients. That is why applying any theoretical model or therapeutic strategy as if it were standardized can lead to misunderstandings. Ask any client who decides not to return to counseling after a session or two, and the most common reason will likely be some variation of "The counselor just didn't get me."

"Integrating cultural context into my work," Leah Brew states with passion, "is probably the most important secret that informs what I do." Brew is herself biracial and specializes in teaching cultural diversity classes in a department in which the vast majority of students are people of color. "I see so many aspects of people's assumptions and behaviors that are culturally constructed. Furthermore, I invite others to tell me their stories, their perspectives. More importantly, though, when I make a racial/ethnic, religious, ability-based, gender-based, or other microaggression, I try to own it well. It does not matter what my intention was when I stated or did something offensive. What matters to me is that I can hear how I have been received and with a full heart offer a sincere apology to repair the damage."

It takes courage to admit that no matter how hard we try or how committed we are to honoring diversity, we cannot help but occasionally become caught up in our own values and preferences. Each of us has our preferences and parameters of familiarity. We all have biases that reflect our most cherished beliefs.

Brew realizes that she has power and authority and can appear intimidating to others, which makes it more difficult for others to provide feedback regarding anything she might say or do that is off-putting. "When this happens, I feel honored that I was safe enough to confront, especially knowing my position of power, and I have the privilege to repair the relationship. I make a conscious effort to understand my clients' and students' culture and the ways they experience their culture." Brew's lesson and secret is that she tries to challenge her assumptions about stereotypes and, even when they seem to fit, remind herself that they might be valid only some of the time, for just selective behaviors. "People are dynamic," she concludes. "We are not static. So we all have the ability to move through the world in inconsistent ways, but ways which are meaningful in their contexts."

Challenging Personal Assumptions and Colonized Discourse

Mayra Martinez works a lot with caregivers and has learned over time that her clients face particular limitations and challenges that require her to operate much differently than she would otherwise. Many of her clients are undocumented immigrants and are terrified of being deported if authorities are in any way involved. They are afraid of even calling the police when their safety is jeopardized, so they call Martinez instead to intervene. This is a part of her job that she never imagined would come to pass.

Miguel Gallardo, introduced earlier, also views his work and efforts as contextualized within the multiple social and cultural identities of his clients. "My work is relational, our lives our relational, and our work needs to be relational as well. Many devalued communities that I work with heal in connection with others and get worse in isolation. I would argue that this is true for most human beings but will reserve comments to my experiences with lower socioeconomic Latino/Latina communities." He has found that in that context the more traditional models, based mostly on privileged, middle-class clients within the majority culture, are not very useful. "Because of this, my work must be liberatory in practice, which translates into me always identifying the strengths and resources clients bring to the healing process, regardless of where they come from, their class status, skin color, and so on. In addition, I always look for ways in which people heal themselves, whether it was one week ago, one month ago, or years ago."

Gallardo points out that most of his clients have been told that they are second-class citizens. More recently, they have been scolded by certain political leaders that they are not welcome and that their contributions are not valued. Gallardo thus sees one of his jobs as to negotiate, mediate, and reframe this colonized discourse. "My own personal and professional processes provide me with an avenue to create paths of consciousness that are cultural, social, and political as a means of resisting imprisonment by false ideologies and beliefs about who the world says I am and who my family is. I believe I must do the same for my clients. If I do not, my healing approach is limited and thus inadequate."

Gallardo acknowledges that as a Mexican American from Texas, now residing in California, teaching at private, expensive university, his clients perceive him in particular ways that both limit and empower him. He wonders continuously about how his own multiple cultural identities shape how he thinks, how he feels, and what he does. "Cultural humility demands that we approach our work with transparency, authenticity, and honesty. This is not authenticity based on what some theory has informed us we should do, but authenticity based on our shared human experiences and connectedness."

The human connectedness and relational engagement that Gallardo speaks of with such eloquence is illustrated in a case mentioned by Ryan Neace, who was also introduced earlier. His client, Everett, was an elderly African American man who had been referred by an attorney. Although Neace had a fair bit of experience with diverse clients, he wondered whether the race and age gap would become an impediment between them. Yet his first impression was that his new client was a charismatic, savvy, successful, easy-going businessman. During their initial session, which lasted 2 hours, Everett described his intense depression and despair after losing his popular restaurant to a fire that had actually been ignited out of negligence by the local fire department during an inspection. The restaurant was uninsured, and so he lost his life's work. As if that weren't enough of a crushing blow, Everett launched a new successful business at an advanced age, only to find himself the victim of fraud that once again destroyed his dream.

"What am I going to do now?" he sobbed. "I have nothing left. And I'm too old to start again."

Neace found it challenging enough just to hold himself together after hearing one of the most tragic runs of misfortune he could imagine. "By this point, I was damn near sobbing myself," he remembers. "Tears were streaming down my face. Everett was holding the kind of pain you can only identify with if you've ever been profoundly broken by life or circumstance, curled up in a fetal position and hurting so badly you can't even muster the strength or focus to wish for death. It's all consuming."

Neace conceptualizes his counseling self like a bucket that he brings to each session. "That bucket is filled with my own pain, which years of counseling and recovery work, growth and maturity, have rendered mostly empty, transforming it into a vessel capable of holding others' pain. Typically the bucket fills up during a day's worth of sessions, and within a day or two it is mostly empty again."

In that first conversation with Everett, the bucket filled to the brim almost immediately, so much so that Neace found himself bringing in reinforcement containers to hold the overflow. It felt like both of them were drowning, bailing just as fast they could. "The only thing to comfort us in our mutual suffering and bewilderment was our interlocked hands and our simple solidarity—his willingness to share his story and my willingness to listen, even if it meant the whole thing might swallow us both up."

Neace felt so privileged that Everett had allowed himself to be seen so vulnerably by this young White guy who was still a stranger. That willingness to be so open was what encouraged Neace to match that level of intimacy and engagement that transcended their cultural differences. There was no real secret to this other than being absolutely, completely present with another, "to lead with myself and allow myself to feel his pain as well as my own. In those moments, as we floated in there together, it felt as though all the pain of marginalized and oppressed peoples, of anyone who has ever had grave injustice committed against them, of anyone who could not find recourse for themselves even when profoundly wronged came crashing down."

Neace wept with his client. And he cried all the way home. He cried that night before bed. He cried off and on for weeks afterward, feeling sorrow for Everett, for himself, and for so many others. He was crying as he told this story.

"I was emotionally hungover for the next several weeks, feeling scattered and weepy. During subsequent sessions with Everett, I was spacey and had difficulty concentrating. And yet at the end of our time together, Everett told me that he'd known it was me he needed to come and see." It didn't matter to Everett that Neace was younger and of a different race and culture; he had researched him online and had felt that they would still be compatible, that sometimes there are more important things than skin color or age differences.

This brings up the point that with all the emphasis in our field, and in the wider culture, to focus on cultural differences, what may be lost in the process is an acknowledgment of shared experiences and universal connections. One of the secrets of exceptional professionals in any field is their willingness and ability to reach across the usual boundaries and barriers that divide us into tribes, types, and cultural entities. We may not know what it's like to grow up in poverty or wealth, to encounter racism or homophobia or bullying, to be disabled or unemployed, to have been undocumented or a refugee, but the best among us can connect with almost anyone in such a way that they feel respected, if not mostly understood.

CHAPTER 8

There Are No Difficult Clients, Only Difficult Counselors

One of the most frequent complaints by counselors is that their clients are resistant, reluctant, difficult, or otherwise uncooperative. It sometimes boggles our minds how people can be so self-sabotaging, eventually undermining any progress accomplished in sessions. Clients lie through their teeth or fail to reveal significant material related to their predicament. They will resolutely declare that they are willing to do most anything to fix a problem and then refuse to take care of the business that is required. They will readily agree to accomplish some task between sessions or complete assigned homework and then "forget" to do so. Of course one of the problems might be that the task was assigned instead of determined by the client, but that's another situation altogether. Regardless of those, there is still sometimes a disconnect between stated desires and follow-through. This could be for all kinds of reasons—ambivalence about change, avoidance of hard work, acting out, buying time—but it is often the consequence of being asked to do things that are beyond one's capability, at least in that moment in time.

I've spent a fair amount of time exploring and writing about the most challenging cases that counselors face in their work. I've interviewed hundreds of practitioners, as well as many of the most prominent theoreticians, to ask them about those clients with whom they struggle the most. Ask most counselors about their difficult clients and you will likely hear a familiar refrain: those with addictions or impulse disorders; those with florid personality disorders; malcontents and complainers; the privileged and entitled; the chronically depressed; the incessantly anxious; individuals consumed with despair and hopelessness; belligerent adolescents; those who ramble, play games, deceive, deny, or destroy things on their own terms. And yet, and yet . . . it's also interesting to consider that so-called difficult clients are really in the eye of the beholder, as each of us deals with our own ghosts, weaknesses, triggers, and limitations.

I used to do workshops called Working With Difficult Clients that followed a book of a similar title, and they were always packed: Everyone wanted to talk about their worst cases, those that drove them crazy. I'd ask participants to meet in small groups and discuss their most challenging case. I remember once doing the program in a smaller community in which all sorts of professionals showed up—hairstylists, realtors, sales personnel, even a few counselors who frantically signaled me to come over for a consult. Apparently each of them had been discussing their most difficult client until they realized they were all describing the same person: This man had been secretly visiting three different counselors without telling any of them—and they all happened to end up in the same group!

My secret, however, is that I don't believe that there are many actual difficult clients in the world, or at least not nearly as many as practitioners would have us believe with all the complaints and competition about whose practice is most challenging. The truth of the matter is that most of the time our clients are just doing the best they can. Are they annoying at times? Of course. That's why they were sent to us in the first place—because they often have trouble getting along with others. But to call them names like *resistant, obstructive,* even *hateful* just because they aren't cooperating the way we prefer says more about us than it does about them. I never quite had the courage to announce this at the beginning of the workshops (or the book), but I think that most of the time the conflicts we encounter are the result of our own inflexibility, our own unrealistic expectations, and the unreasonable demands we make on people with which they are not yet ready—or able—to comply.

Be Careful What You Ask People

One secret I learned along the way is to avoid asking clients to do things they are either not yet ready to do or unable to do. In fact, one conception of so-called difficult or challenging clients is that they are those who are not meeting our own expectations. It is sometimes the case that they simply can't manage to accomplish whatever it was they said (or we said) they would do.

"I really meant to do the homework," the client offers apologetically. "But some things just came up and I never really got around to it."

"You mean you decided not to follow through even though you mentioned in the last session that it was so important."

"No, that's not it at all! It *is* important to me. Please believe me. But you know, I have other responsibilities that I have to . . ."

"Some other priorities, you mean."

"Well, that too. But I really do want to work on this. It's just hard to find the time."

We can readily see where this conversation is going, and it's clear that both people are frustrated with each other. The client feels criticized, blamed, and shamed for not doing what was promised, and the counselor feels frustrated because things are not proceeding according to the plan that was agreed on. At the heart of this misunderstanding, however, is that the client isn't yet prepared to proceed at the pace that the counselor prefers. In one sense, all such difficult clients really are trying to cooperate with the treatment: They are just doing so at a pace and style that is different from what the counselor might prefer.

It is often the case that our own impatience, or perhaps cherished ideas, leads us to push and cajole clients to do things that they clearly are not prepared to do. They may like the *idea* of such action. They are certainly persuaded that it would be good for them, perhaps even life changing. They absolutely intend to try out what has been discussed and actually mean to keep that promise at the time. But then situations are not exactly like what was anticipated. The timing isn't quite right. Things are so much harder than they should be. And then when the excuses run out, there's just a shrug: "Sorry, I just couldn't do it."

Although it appears as if the client is accepting responsibility for negligence or laziness or even cowardice, it is equally possible that the counselor should be the one to consider that what was prescribed may not have been the most appropriate option at the time. I don't know about you, but it does feel frustrating to just sit and listen to someone drone on and on about the same problems, week after week, seemingly unwilling to do much to change the predicament. That's when my own impatience kicks in, when I am inclined to think, if not say aloud, "Okay, enough is enough! Stop the damn complaining all the time. Let's talk about what you can actually do to extricate yourself from this situation instead of feeling like such a victim."

I admit, that's a bit harsh. And I likely wouldn't say such a thing quite as unfiltered as that. But that's not to say I wouldn't be *thinking* something similar, feeling helpless and useless because there has been so little noticeable change in the client's life. He still feels just as stuck as ever, and now he's sucked me into the muck as well. He may have given up struggling, content to accept his swampy lot, but I got into this profession in the first place because I believe so strongly in the power to change. And this dude is definitely not cooperating!

Counselors can and do become triggered by what is encountered during sessions. Most of us have worked pretty hard to attain some semblance of emotional stability if not exceptional well-being. We like the idea of personal power to change. We believe strongly that almost anything is possible, given enough conviction, preparation, skills, resources, and support. So it can be challenging for us to allow others to remain mired in their misery, especially when we believe that we have the tools to help them choose a different path when they are ready to do so. But it is also really about when *we* are ready to do so.

One example of the dangers of asking clients to do things for which they aren't yet ready or prepared is shared by Dora, who works in a recovery facility. Many of the women she works with are transitioning out of the agency even though they continue to work as prostitutes in order to obtain money for drugs. She'd estimate that about 80% of them are stuck in that cycle.

Dora struggles helplessly as she often observes her clients continue to ruin their lives with some of the ongoing bad choices they make. She is justifiably concerned about the ways in which these women are exploited and abused, and she often finds herself arguing with some of her clients, trying to convince them to follow an altogether different path. It took her awhile to realize that pushing them to give up a $700-per-hour job in exchange for minimum wage was probably not the best case she could make. Dora realized that one of the hardest things she has to do is demonstrate patience until her clients are ready to fully complete the transition to a different life.

Of course we do far more than just sit around waiting for clients to decide that they are finally ready to convert talk into action. Regardless of one's preferred therapeutic orientation, whether it favors explicit readiness approaches like motivational interviewing or more indirect insight-oriented theories, the goal is to help people to feel increasingly uncomfortable and dissatisfied with their current predicament. Until such time that their favored coping strategies no longer work to postpone constructive action, we nudge them along by helping them to more clearly face the consequences of their behavior. Nevertheless, some people seem to take an extraordinarily infuriating amount of time to get moving.

Blame the Client

It's not much of a secret at all that one game we counselors play is to blame the client when outcomes are less than satisfactory. There are some legitimate reasons for this of course, especially considering that unless clients feel some incentive, motivation, and determination to make needed changes, our therapeutic options become far more limited. Indeed, the single best predictor of a successful outcome is directly related to client characteristics such as resilience, hardiness, motivation, and the particular attitudes they bring to sessions.

Although I acknowledge that certainly clients bear considerable responsibility for the success of their counseling, it is also to be expected that we as professionals share some of the blame as well when things don't go well. But notice how often we complain in meetings, in supervision, or with peers about how uncooperative and resistant particular clients might be. Why can't they get with the program? Why do they have to play such games? Why do they continue to make our jobs so much harder than they need to be?

It's interesting the different ways that practitioners make sense of so-called impasses or resistance. We can tell ourselves the person just isn't ready to change and shrug our shoulders as if we've got all the time in the world. We can point to particular defenses that are slowing the process down. We can label and diagnose all kinds of what we call *obstructive behavior.* We can blame forces outside of our control, all perfectly reasonable—the economy, family meddling, past trauma, institutional policies, limited time or resources, even bad luck.

Then there are other practitioners who might end up on the other end of the continuum, blaming *themselves* for anything that goes wrong. If only they were better trained, more intelligent, or more perceptive and insightful . . . If only they hadn't said or done . . . If only they had been more patient, or forceful, or . . .

Although it is true that the most exceptional counselors still fail and make mistakes on occasion, even lose a few clients because of some misjudgment or miscalculation, one distinguishing feature of their internal processing is that they are willing to strike a balance between assessing the client's counterproductive behavior and also honestly and critically considering their own contributions to the problem. After all, we are well versed in the dynamics of relational conflict, and it is *never* just one person's fault.

Instead of blaming the client for being obstructive, defensive, or resistant, John Murphy prefers to find sources of leverage to make a deeper relational connection. This helps him not to view particular clients as difficult or necessarily challenging so much as requiring a different or higher degree of creativity and flexibility. As an example, Murphy recalls an 11-year-old boy he was asked by a school principal to help. Ronald had been somewhat belligerent, arguing with teachers, fighting with other students, disrupting class, and refusing to do his schoolwork. In short, this might have been the prototypical case of the reluctant or difficult client.

Murphy often video records his sessions, assuming of course that the kids and their guardians approve of the procedure. He explains to them that it helps him to review sessions afterward so he can better prepare for subsequent meetings. When Ronald entered the art supply room that Murphy was using as an office in the school, Murphy immediately asked him for help cleaning up the art materials that were scattered on the table. Murphy wondered whether Ronald knew anything about recorders and perhaps could help him set up the camera. Murphy shrugged sheepishly, as if to apologize for his technological ignorance even if it was exaggerated.

"Do you know how to work this thing?" Murphy asked while pointing to the camera.

Rather than answering directly, Ronald started tinkering with the device, assembling pieces on the tripod, experimenting with some of the buttons.

"Oh," Murphy frequently said. "Now I see what you're doing. But what is this thing for, and what does it do?"

When Ronald answered, Murphy remarked how impressed he was with this advanced knowledge. "How do you know these things?" Murphy asked him. "I mean, how do you know how things work?"

"I don't know. I just do."

"Well, I really appreciate you helping me out with this. Okay, let's get started."

Of course they had gotten started already, as Murphy was using one of his favorite methods for engaging so-called difficult adolescents: He was recruiting Ronald's help by turning the tables on their relationship. It had begun with the video recorder but next involved other areas.

"I'm curious," Murphy asked Ronald once they began talking about the school situation. "You seem to know and understand so much about the teachers in this school who seem to give students a hard time—or at least it sometimes feels that way to you. I wonder what advice you would give to other students who are having the same kinds of frustrations and difficulties that you are."

Ronald studied Murphy to see whether he was serious. Once he was convinced that this was a legitimate request, not intended to ridicule him, Ronald reeled off a long list of ideas and suggestions, more than Murphy could have ever imagined.

"Those are some remarkable ideas, I agree," Murphy told him. "And what do you think that *you* need to do to get everyone off your case at school?"

"You mean take my own advice?"

"Exactly!"

The two of them then put their heads together to settle on a few simple things that Ronald could do to reduce the difficulties he was facing every day. Although he didn't dramatically transform his behavior overnight, Ronald did improve sufficiently that he managed to advance to the next grade level.

This Can You Help Me? strategy reminds Murphy that there are so many different ways to connect with clients who at first don't seem very cooperative. His secret is to level the relationship as much as he can, to distribute power and control more evenly, so that some clients don't feel the need to obstruct the process because they feel like they are in charge.

On Demonstrating Flexibility and Adaptability in the Face of So-Called Resistance

One of the most challenging aspects of working with certain clients is that they are not willing—or able—to function according to our usual, customary, and preferred expectations. They don't play by our rules. They appear difficult precisely because they don't fit well into the established structures of their worlds, whether at home, school, or work. It is not that they are obstructive because they want to be, but rather they have at times been exposed to life experiences, trauma, abuse, or suffering that is so far out of the bounds of what we can even imagine.

Consider those clients with whom you have struggled the most, the ones you have found most frustrating and challenging to help. I've spent considerable time interviewing counselors about these cases, and the consistent responses are probably no surprise. Those individuals who are most often mentioned include the following:

- Angry, belligerent adolescents
- Clients who are mute or won't talk at all, even when prompted
- Substance abusers who won't admit the extent of their indulgence
- Clients who are deceptive, manipulative, and overly controlling
- Clients who talk a good game during session but don't follow through
- Children whose parents constantly meddle in the sessions

- Families that are so toxic and dysfunctional that the norms seem impervious to change
- Those with personality configurations that lean toward narcissistic or sociopathic
- Clients who act out or consistently miss or cancel appointments, always with feeble excuses
- Clients with impulse disorders that lead to continuously self-destructive behavior
- Clients who have experienced trauma or abuse so profound and deep that it seems impossible to get through
- Clients who are argumentative, even abusive at times
- Individuals who externalize blame and refuse to accept responsibility for their behavior
- People who ramble incessantly and rarely actually listen
- Clients who become so overly dependent that it seems like they will never let go
- Those with a hidden agenda that has nothing to do with wanting to get better or change
- Clients who display depression, despair, and hopelessness so extreme and unresponsive to any medication that the feelings are contagious
- Clients who know how to push your buttons or trigger your own unresolved issues

Well, you get the point. This is only a mere sampling of those kinds of cases that might be mentioned. I've found it interesting not that there might be some consensus regarding which clients may be experienced as most challenging but rather how often we might differ in our perceptions. I once worked with a partner, Diane, who specialized in working with young children, whereas I especially enjoyed working with adolescents. We had a discussion one day about how and why we had ended up with these sorts of practices considering that they seemed to just evolve that way over time. Then we figured out that Diane had three adolescent children at home and I was the father of a 3-year-old. Neither one of us wanted to work with kids the same age as our own because we were so exhausted doing so at home. Our solution was that I referred young children to her while she sent adolescents to me, thus avoiding the cases we found most exhausting.

Daya Singh Sandhu considers one of his most important secrets when working with any so-called difficult client is to not surrender or give up in the face of someone who is uncooperative, angry, stubborn, or otherwise resistant. Resist the urge to become complacent, cop out, or refer to someone else and instead fuel greater imagination and proactivity. He mentions as an example Leslie, a 17-year-old Choctaw Indian who was incredibly angry, disruptive, and even violent and had been referred by the principal of her school as a last resort before expulsion. In particular, Sandhu was saddled with the responsibility of writing a report on the girl's aggressive and aggravating behavior and sorting out the reasons for her seemingly inexplicable actions.

"Leslie appeared quite overwhelmed, sad, agitated, and belligerent when I invited her to my office," Sandhu explains. "She didn't exchange greetings and just dropped into a chair with an exasperated sigh. Despite my repeated requests, she refused to answer any questions about her presenting problems. And yet she appeared quite distraught as she stared at the floor." It was at this point that Sandhu realized that any sort of typical conversation or engagement wasn't going to be very useful and was likely only to further frustrate both of them. Instead, he invited her into another room for a drink of water, in part to give himself time to consider other options.

There was no immediate breakthrough, but Sandhu realized that the secret to engaging with this girl, or any rather unusual client, was that there was no secret. Each case is totally unique, requiring some sort of mutually negotiated means of connection. He tried an assortment of different things, some fruitful but most failing miserably. Nevertheless, because they both seemed stuck with each other, over a period of weeks Leslie eventually let leak out some of the things that had been going on in her life. Maybe she felt sorry for him, but a few days after a particularly frustrating interaction between them she brought him a sealed envelope containing a 7-page letter describing some of the traumatic events of her young life. Her mother had been killed by a drunk driver when she was just an infant. Her mother's sister had raised her until age 5, when she had then died of breast cancer (talk about abandonment issues!). Her biological father—who had also abandoned her—had been murdered 2 years later. She was then passed on to her elderly grandmother, who also passed on just a few years later. She ended up in foster care during the next few years, raped at age 15 and moving from one household to the next, one trauma after another. Sandhu considered it an absolute miracle that she was actually doing as well as she was considering all the disappointments, tragedies, neglect, and abuse she'd suffered.

Sandhu's relationship with Leslie was a powerfully influential experience in his own development as a counselor. "It occurred to me there really are no problem children, only problem parents and caretakers. Whereas effective parenting involves encouraging and facilitating the development of healthy, well-adjusted children who are prepared to deal with the vicissitudes of life, children raised by problem parents often become alienated, frustrated, confused, and violent. There are no emotional ties of love that anchor these children to any authority figure who may provide them with hope, support, and guidance." Sandhu further explains that children like Leslie eventually internalize their pain, developing maladaptive worldviews. "Their minds become preoccupied with negative thoughts and fantasies. Memories of past traumatic events relating to abuse or neglect may lead them to develop cruel indifference toward others and suffer from inner confusion." This realization became a powerful insight for Sandhu, a secret that has helped to guide his work, especially with regard to clients who aren't willing to speak verbally, requiring him to adapt the mode of communication and connection to respect and honor the client's readiness level. In Leslie's case, she needed time to trust her counselor enough to decide that she was willing to speak through a letter.

Outside Influences on the Therapeutic Relationship

Kayla and her husband first consulted me because they were both concerned about some health issues related to her "obesity." It struck me right away that although Kayla did look a bit overweight, it certainly did not seem to qualify as excessive. She was a strikingly beautiful woman who just seemed to be rather large boned. Nevertheless, they both declared that her main priority was to begin an effective diet plan because nothing they had tried previously had been effective.

At the time, I was experimenting with a strategy for weight loss that had nothing to do with diets or even particular food choices because the compelling evidence seemed to be that all diets work—for a little while—and then the efforts inevitably fail because it is virtually impossible to maintain the regimen indefinitely. You can restrain yourself from eating favorite foods for a few months, or practice self-restraint for a period of time, but often the diet's restrictions are so incongruent with the realities of daily life. Besides, why would someone want to go through life without chocolate or favorite snacks?

My usual weight-loss program was to instruct clients that they could actually eat anything they wanted, whenever they wanted, as long as they wrote it down 1 day ahead of time. They were only permitted to eat something if they had the foresight to plan for it. They had to be as specific as possible, detailing exact quantities of items (11 M&Ms or four spoonfuls of mashed potatoes with butter and sour cream). In other words, rather than forbidding themselves from eating their favorite foods, which leads to cravings, they could have anything—but always in moderation and with advanced planning. It was almost foolproof, and it worked perfectly for Kayla as well. Several weeks in a row she reported consistent, gradual progress. It did seem peculiar, however, that during sessions while she was animated and proud, her husband seemed glum and less than enthusiastic.

They cancelled the next few appointments. When I saw them next, the two of them were barely speaking at all. "She just doesn't care about her health, or even about me," the husband reported in a pouting tone with his arms crossed. "She's just fat and I can barely look at her." He paused and then added, "I have no interest in her sexually when she looks like that."

It turned out, after considerable exploration, that what had actually changed was the exact opposite of what the husband was reporting. Kayla had been making wonderful progress toward her goals, that is until her husband started actively sabotaging her efforts. Apparently as she was losing weight, he began to notice that other men were paying far more attention to her, and he was feeling increasingly threatened by this. In truth, he really wanted her to stay as she was so he could continually control her and protect himself from his own insecurities. So he started deliberately leaving enticing, forbidden foods around the house that he knew were not on her daily list. In spite of what he said, he was doing everything in his power to sabotage any progress.

Of course we see this sort of thing all the time, in which it seems like a client is being resistant or difficult when in fact there are larger forces at work. The ideas of triangulation, circular causality, coalitions, family legacies, cultural colonization, scripts, and similar dynamics are now accepted as standard forces that operate powerfully to affect the ways in which people change, or at least try to do so. As much as we may have been trained in family systems thinking, it is still only one of several different external factors that must be understood and managed.

Chris Williams found in his research interviewing therapists that one of his main realizations was to come to terms with the reality that we really don't have as much control and power as we think. It's kind of ridiculous to expect that spending an hour per week with someone is going to somehow counteract all the other negative influences, distractions, and entrenched habits in his or her life.

When Williams asked practitioners about the main obstacles they faced in their work, almost all of them mentioned the ways in which outside influences such as friends and family members may try to sabotage or compromise progress. Another variation on this theme was mentioned by counselors who specialized in working with couples and noted how challenging it sometimes is to help them when they keep undermining each other every chance they get. Still one more example was reported by counselors who worked with young children and had to deal with parents or guardians who would refuse to look at their own role in creating the problems.

And then there is organizational bureaucracy as an impediment, limiting what we are permitted to do, even if it is not necessarily in the client's best interests. There are policies that restrict how long we can see clients, what diagnoses we can assess that are actually approved for reimbursement, and even which treatment strategies are sanctioned and which are not approved. Finally, perhaps the most challenging outside influence of all might be our own colleagues, administrators, and supervisors. This job is hard enough as it is without having to navigate the complex political swamps that exist in many organizations, agencies, and schools.

Rules of Engagement With Challenging Clients

One of the secrets that many counselors have realized when confronting seemingly intractable or frustrating cases is to first separate clients' behavior from their own issues that may be getting in the way. I'm not just speaking about countertransference in its traditional sense but about all the ways that our personalities, needs, values, preferences, values, and moods might be making things far more difficult than they need to be. It is for this reason that when I feel stuck, or when I notice that things aren't proceeding well at all (which means I first have to notice this, which isn't always obvious), I ask myself a series of uncomfortable questions:

- What am I doing to create or exacerbate the problems?
- Who does the client remind me of that is blocking my ability to see him or her as he or she is?
- What personal issues of mine are being triggered by our interactions together?
- How am I acting out my impatience with the client's lack of apparent progress?
- What expectations am I demanding of this client that he or she is unable or unwilling to meet?
- What needs of mine are not being met, especially those related to recognition, approval, and feelings of competence?

Of course just because I'm asking these questions doesn't mean I have the answers, at least at the time. It does signal, however, that it's time for me to get back to work on myself, just as I expect from my clients.

Now that we've acknowledged that the perception of difficult clients is actually an interactive, relational phenomenon, subject as much to the counselor's behavior and reactions as those of the client, it is also important to mention that certain rules of engagement kick in once we recognize that we are dealing with someone who is, let us say, a bit unusual in our experience. If, for example, we recognize that a client is displaying florid symptoms and manipulative behavior of a toxic personality, we would enforce clear relational boundaries to maintain a more restrained holding environment. The challenge for us is to maintain a degree of empathic engagement and compassion while at the same time instituting some self-protective measures to counteract attempts to penetrate our own defenses.

Another often helpful secret is to remind ourselves to stop complaining. So often when counselors get together, we compete with one another about who has the most bizarre or challenging cases. Or we seek sympathy from others because we feel like victims of ingratitude or abuse. We might get plenty of sympathy and support, but it only ends up reinforcing our sense of futility and frustration. My secret, when I remember, is to repeat the following mantra to myself: "The client is only doing his job. My client is only doing his job. It's his job to be the way he is. It's his job to keep behaving in this way. That's why he was sent to me in the first place."

Still another rule of engagement once a client or a relationship has been identified as challenging is sometimes to do less rather than more. With difficult cases, we often dig in and work harder to make a difference when initial efforts fail. It's one of those admonishments I recall from many supervisors of the past: "Never work harder than your clients." When I notice I'm talking too much in session, when I become aware that I'm thinking too much about a particular client between sessions, when I feel almost a level of desperation to help someone, I realize that I have too much at stake and I have to force myself to back off and take a breath. Usually it is once again my impatience getting in the way.

It's also important to get support when we feel stuck. I'm not just referring to bringing the case to supervision, which is always a first option; I'm assuming that has already been tried a few times without noticeable effect. There are times when I've recognized that a difficult counseling relationship is very much like any dysfunctional couple and requires some sort of mediation. On occasion I've actually said this to a client and asked whether it might be helpful to bring in another counselor to help us resolve our impasse or difficulty. Even if this offer is declined, clients seem to appreciate that I'm framing the conflict as a shared responsibility.

There are so many other rules of engagement that may also be useful during challenging cases or with resistant clients. It often helps to focus more on accentuating the positive and focusing on even minimal gains rather than continuously lamenting what is not working. It's important to also keep our sense of humor: Sometimes the extent to which some clients will go to make themselves (and others) miserable is not only tragic but also ridiculous in its own way.

Finally, it's often useful to just let go, surrender, to what we can't control and change. I don't mean that we give up, but we more realistically accept the realities of a given case, what is possible and what is not. It is so-called difficult or challenging cases that teach us the most, not only about the nature of change and its avoidance but also about ourselves. It is when we feel stuck or stymied that we are most inclined to explore more deeply what it is that we do that is most and least helpful.

CHAPTER 9

Boundaries Opaque and Permeable

Let's be honest: Surely one reason why a reader would pick up a book that promises "secrets" of exceptional counselors would be to learn a few new tricks and pick up a few pointers that will only further empower therapeutic work. We are all hungry for the latest, best techniques and the most innovative cutting-edge interventions to increase our effectiveness. Participants of any workshop or conference crave their handouts, believing that that they will hold in their hands sacred information that will finally reveal the hidden secrets of the masters.

Whatever latest tools, technology, or (supposed) transformational strategy arrives on the market attracts immediate attention as The Answer to all our troubles and therapeutic stalemates. Move your fingers back and forth. Hook up physiological feedback instruments. Access somatic neuroprocessing data. Incorporate mindfulness-based imagery. Introduce applied behavior analysis. Throw in a few metaphors or reconstructed narratives. Try some traumatic debriefing or hypnotic inductions. The list goes on and on—all the intriguing, sometimes desperate attempts to master the best, latest, most powerful new techniques that will render obsolete all we have previously known.

Honoring the Client's Theory of Change

On some level, we know and understand all the research and evidence that flies in the face of the belief that specific techniques even matter. Thousands of studies demonstrative conclusively and overwhelmingly that success in counseling (or in the larger world for that matter) is about the quality of the relationships we enjoy. It is the closest thing to a fact that we might hold onto in a discipline in which there are sometimes few irrefutable truths.

As mentioned previously, Barry Duncan has devoted most of his career to researching the factors that contribute most to successful outcomes. Given the compelling evidence he has collected and analyzed, he is absolutely committed to making sure the alliance is as strong as possible—and that is his greatest secret. "Most of us are pretty good at a few of the features of the alliance," Duncan explains, "namely, the relational bond, which ensures that the client perceives and acknowledges our empathy, authenticity, and unconditional positive regard." Yet he feels that another issue is also critical: agreement on the part of both counselor and client(s) regarding the goals of sessions and how counseling will best address these issues. Duncan believes that all too often counselors may neglect or forget the critical importance of negotiating the choices and decisions made. "Most times clients get what the counselor has to offer without much negotiation. This is probably our biggest alliance blind spot despite growing evidence that matching client preferences and collaborating about the methods of therapy increase the chances of a positive outcome."

Duncan considers this not only a neglected secret of our work but an example of how and why many of our investigations have been misdirected to focus on matching supposed optimal interventions or favored theories with designated disorders instead of looking at the bigger picture of what clients actually report means the most to them. And guess what *that* is?

Clients will forgive us for all sorts of mistakes and misjudgments as long as they believe that we are listening and understand them. I will mention that again because it is so important: It doesn't seem to matter whether we really understand our clients or not—which is a good thing considering how rare it is that we ever understand ourselves, much less anyone else. What matters most is that they *feel* understood by us.

Duncan talks about this phenomenon as an example of the "client's theory of change," which he actually considers more important than our own preferred model. Unless we are willing and able to meet clients where they are, they will just leave us behind or reject whatever it is that we offer them. This might seem like a little thing, not much of a big secret at all, but Duncan thinks that is imperative that we validate the client's experience of what may be helpful.

When I talk about boundaries related to the counseling relationship, the discussion is usually couched in the language of ethical violations and so-called boundary violations. Yet there are also boundary crossings that do not necessarily lead to some ethical breach or disastrous outcome. Much depends on the reasons and context for the variation of the standard treatment protocol that takes place in an office in which two people sit facing each other in chairs. If Duncan and others are correct, the relationship is *everything* and it is best constructed based not just on what counselors prefer and like but also on what is in the best interests of a given client.

This leads to another secret related to this subject. Although I have previously written about famous therapists who engaged in all kinds of rather unusual relational adaptations, most practitioners tend to keep such experimental strategies under wraps for fear of critical judgment. There are reasons of course why we have prohibitions against self-indulgent or careless relational configurations that jeopardize client safety. Nevertheless, there are times when clients would feel so much more open and comfortable if some of the standard rules are not so much put aside as adapted. Examples of this are when counselors might conduct home visits, take children outside to play, or be more personally disclosing than usual because the situation calls for a closer, more authentic connection. The key is that this is done not for convenience but rather because it is what the client needs most.

Relational Protections and Transformations

One of the foundations of our profession is to protect the safety and care of our clients, especially from any inadvertent, unintentional, or even deliberate exploitation. In extreme cases, some clients have been emotionally, even sexually, abused by their counselors; other times clients might be exposed to counselors' indulgences when the latter self-disclose too extensively or otherwise meet their own needs during sessions. It is for this reason that clear boundaries have been defined and enforced to minimize such lapses or boundary violations.

It's more than a little ironic that the whole notion of such strict parameters began with Sigmund Freud's earliest work during the very inception of counseling as a professional enterprise distinct from the other rather strange treatments that were available at the time, such as animal magnetism and addictive drugs. Freud became tired of having his clients stare at him all day long and so decided that if they reclined on a couch, it might not only better facilitate free association but also provide him with a bit more privacy.

As mentioned, a distinction has been made between boundary violations and those adjustments that are considered in the client's own best interests. The latter may involve greater flexibility in how and where counseling is delivered but do not overtly either meet the counselor's needs or involve exploitation of and danger to a client in any way.

Like most traditionally trained counselors, I was warned repeatedly to maintain strict boundaries in my therapeutic work. I was taught the importance of always beginning and ending sessions exactly on time as part of the holding environment to provide consistently maintained and predicted behavior to act as a grounding. During my practicum, my instructor was so scrupulous about enforcing time boundaries that he demanded that we end sessions *exactly* after 50 minutes, plus or minus 30 seconds. At 45 minutes after the hour, he would knock on the door, signaling that there were 5 minutes left. If more than 30 seconds elapsed beyond the appointed time, he would open the door and stare at me and my client. Needless to say, that was so humiliating that I learned to be absolutely obsessed with starting on time and ending exactly on time. To this day, I still practice this in the classroom as soon as I see the sweep-hand of seconds on the clock approach the hour.

I also learned the importance of creating and enforcing the kind of atmosphere that would provide a secure environment for deep exploration. That's one reason I would begin and end sessions the same way, sit in the same place each time, and introduce a pattern that would become dependable over time. I could even hear myself begin and end counseling the exact same way each time: "Our time's up. Let's summarize what happened today. When would you like to reschedule?"

My doctoral internship took place in an adult psychiatric clinic of a university hospital, so many of my first clients were somewhat emotionally volatile and displayed severe symptoms of mental disturbance. In other early cases, I discovered far too late that I was dealing with highly manipulative personality disturbances. Thus, out of necessity I became a stickler for relational boundaries, as much to protect myself as for any therapeutic value.

So many decades of practice later, I still maintain that the overriding imperative of our work is to do no harm. I am careful to make certain that my efforts are solely directed to the client's best interests and frequently challenge myself when I think I might be slipping into some form of self-indulgence, perhaps sharing a story that is less than relevant or asking a question just to satisfy my own curiosity. And yet I've interviewed so many therapists and counselors over the years to learn that actual practice, especially in rather unusual or challenging cases, does not necessarily follow a traditional template. Historical luminaries in the field have done all kinds of (what I consider) unusual and perhaps radical things to get through to their clients. I mention these examples with the disclaimer that they are hardly strategies I would recommend or be inclined to use myself. Family theorist Carl Whitaker would sometimes hold clients on his lap. Reality therapist William Glasser went running with a client during sessions to address an eating disorder. Milton Erickson once sat on top of a client to demonstrate issues of power. Gestalt therapist Fritz Perls would provocatively confront clients way beyond what I would consider appropriate. Multimodal theorist Arnold Lazarus once took a client to a bar to teach him how to meet and engage women. Solution-focused therapist Cloé Madanes shared a story with me in which she urged a couple with sexual difficulties to hire a dominatrix to assist them. Although these stories are certainly provocative and interesting, it struck me that only someone who is famous and known for such rather unusual strategies could get away with such a thing without dire consequences. And yet it also got me thinking about the boundaries that are customary and wondering which are truly for the client's best interests and which are for our own convenience.

French psychoanalyst Jacques Lacan thought it ridiculous that we have set an arbitrary time limit of 50 minutes for each session. Where is the evidence that this is the inviolate rule that produces the best outcome? He believed that some people need only 5 minutes for a session (when they are playing games or have little to say), whereas others may need 3 hours of concentrated work when in crisis. And where has it been indelibly written in stone that counseling must take place in an office, sitting in two chairs? After all, healers in most other parts of the world think it utterly ridiculous to believe that having a conversation for an hour in a comfortable setting actually leads to any enduring changes. Indigenous healers, for example, work primarily by conducting home visits, prescribing tasks, and assigning challenging trials for their clients to complete—always in more naturalistic settings.

I've witnessed indigenous healing rituals, the equivalent of counseling in our culture, among the Maoris of New Zealand, Aboriginals of Australia, Quechua of Peru, Bushmen of the Kalahari, and native peoples of North America, among others. I've sat on mountaintops, around community fires, on beaches, and in deserts during therapeutic gatherings with healers. So many of them believe that the real action takes place not via talk but through communal support and real-life tasks that involve risk and commitment. Healers in some African cultures actually move into the homes of their clients so as to better observe behavior and initiate constructive healing; others require their clients to move in with them until a cure takes place. In other words, it is only in our counseling tradition, the youngest healing practice of them all, in which boundaries are conceived so narrowly. And once again, I'm not in any way suggesting that we *ever* do anything that puts our clients at greater risk: After all, the purpose of boundaries in the first place is to install barriers against potential harm.

There are certainly some boundaries that most of us would indeed consider inviolate. For instance, any sexual or emotional seduction is entirely inappropriate and dangerous. Likewise, meeting clients for any kind of social interaction would usually be considered a serious ethical problem. And yet as psychologist Ofer Zur and others have pointed out, there are times when crossing boundaries is actually in the client's best interests, and to refuse to consider this option may actually jeopardize significant and meaningful improvement.

The Value of Experiential Learning and Boundary Considerations

I have led many service and advocacy projects in which students, professionals, and others travel to far-flung places in the world to address issues of trauma, human trafficking, abuse, neglect, and disaster relief. We all live together, staying in very primitive facilities, and are subjected to incredible levels of stress and secondary trauma. Most of the time, someone in the group is crying because they are either so physically challenged or else emotionally flooded by all that is being witnessed and experienced.

Imagine, if you will, entering the home of an adorable 11-year-old girl. She lives with her mother and two brothers in a hut built of stone and mud with a thatched roof. You can barely duck your head through the open door into the darkness. Once your eyes adjust, you see the girl sitting on a pallet, her bed, that she shares with her mother. Her two brothers share another one against the wall. Yet the truly remarkable thing about the setting is how proud the girl is of her home and family.

You sit down next to her and she shows you some of the notebooks in which she has completed her homework. They are difficult to decipher, not just because there is no light in the room but because she has written in such tiny script covering every bit of the pages. When you ask why, she shrugs and tells you that she could only afford one notebook for school.

You are taken aside once you leave and told that although she is the brightest and most capable girl in her class, she will soon be pulled out of school because her mother can no longer afford the minimal fees and supplies that are required to even attend public school. The previous year, her husband (the girl's father) abandoned the family to parts unknown. The mother has been left to struggle on her own, and she can only afford to send her sons to school.

What will happen to this brilliant girl? you wonder. You are told an uncle will find her a job across the border. What this really means is that she will be sold, if she's lucky, to a wealthy family as a domestic slave; more likely it will be to a brothel, where her life expectancy will be about 3 years.

You stumble out of the hut and break out sobbing in despair. You see the girl staring at you with curiosity but you can't help yourself. You feel such despair and hopelessness, such incredible sadness that you can't hold the feelings inside. You are crying for her, for her family, and for yourself and the rest of the world.

The others in your group crowd around you, hold you, hug you, embrace one another. A few others lose control as well, and you are all trying to regain your composure. But it is time to move on to the next home visit. Time to visit another girl in a miserable predicament. Time to figure out what can be done to rescue these children from certain misery.

The person I'm describing, by the way, is *me.* As many years as I've been doing this sort of work around the world, I still sometimes can't contain myself. All of us who are part of the teams are triggered at times, especially the students and counseling interns who are so unprepared for this kind of work in the field with the most marginalized clients imaginable. The usual boundaries that exist in the classroom or in the comfortable confines of an office collapse. There are concerns about one's physical safety as well as psychological stability. It is rather obvious not only that under such circumstances there are lessons to be learned—as well as risks—outside of traditional teaching and supervision but also that such growth and personal and professional development is likely to stick in ways that can't be touched by a textbook, lecture, seminar discussion, or supervision conversation.

Each evening there is usually some processing that very much resembles a counseling group in terms of the depth and kind of sharing. I can say unequivocally that I have never witnessed (or experienced myself) more dramatic and enduring positive growth than has taken place in such a setting with high levels of emotional arousal, a very novel environment, and some adversity. I've become convinced over time that the more unique and different the setting, the more people are selectively and carefully exposed to life challenges, the more emotional and social support offered, the more incredible the changes that take place—far more than could ever occur in a weekly conversation.

Then there are the accidental and incidental situations that arise, leading to the kinds of boundary crossings that would not usually be planned or considered. Anyone who has ever worked with adolescents or children knows full well that some of the best work takes place outside the office. I wish to once again to be clear: I am not advocating that we as counselors start testing and challenging the consensual standards and safeguards of our profession but rather that we consider which boundaries are truly designed to protect clients and which are based on our own personal preferences and convenience.

Thelma Duffey doesn't think it's much of a secret at all to recognize and encourage therapeutic relationships that are far more creative, customized, and responsive to each client's particular needs. "At the end of the day, when we create a space where our clients genuinely represent themselves without fear of judgment or evaluation, and when we have the kind of relationship and empathy that lets clients know we are moved by them and their experiences, we do our best work."

Consistent with her interests in relational-cultural therapy, as well as the creative process in clinical work, Duffey has always been interested in fostering growth within her helping relationships. Within that context, most counselors manage boundaries (hopefully) according to their strategic vision of what is most helpful to a given client rather than merely reflecting personal tastes. There are some clients (think major narcissistic or sociopathic personality styles) with whom we would enforce the strictest possible parameters for sessions without exception. Yet there are other clients (young children, the elderly, survivors of trauma, refugees, etc.) with whom we would expand some of the boundaries in order to accommodate cognitive functioning, the capacity for insight, the need for movement, and so on.

"In my practice," Duffey reveals, "I work with people challenged with various concerns such as addiction, divorce, death, relationship problems, illness, miscarriage, and losses. And yet people go to counseling because they want to function better in life. They don't want to be controlled by old issues, old patterns, or unresolved losses. And they want a counselor to respect them and connect with them and their experiences. We do this in part by being with clients in ways that empower them, in ways that promote self-compassion and that help them know they have a partner in the journey. Sometimes this means helping them revisit their experiences and come to terms with them in a more empowering way."

Echoing this deep commitment to relational connections, perhaps with different boundary enforcement, Brian Van Brunt reflects on the privilege and honor of holding his clients' stories. "I become part of their fear, pain, worry, desire, rage, and hope. They honor me with those fragile, shifting pieces. I turn each fragment of their experience in my mind and push them to embrace a more resilient account of their lives. They offer me the divinity to forgive, absolve, pardon, and care for them. I watch our experience fold together and we both grow stronger. We become more connected to each other and the world around us. My reward is their brief, tentative smile."

Oh, the reward is often far more than a "brief, tentative smile"! Sure, we appreciate acknowledgment and gratitude for our efforts, but far more than that we live to know ourselves that we have made a difference in someone's life.

CHAPTER 10

It Takes Chutzpah

Who are the heroes and heroines you most admire, within both the profession and the larger world? I'm guessing that more likely than not, such individuals have one characteristic in spades—and that's the determination to do whatever it takes to make a difference in people's lives and the community. The mentors, authors, and leaders you respect the most would not take no for an answer when faced with inevitable obstacles or criticism from those who felt threatened by their novel ideas. Sigmund Freud was ostracized within the medical community after articulating his controversial theories. Throughout history, whenever people have demonstrated the mettle to challenge the way things have always been done, they have faced a barrage of attacks by those who have felt threatened.

Look at medical advances as examples. Poor Ignaz Semmelweis, the surgeon who first suggested that his colleagues were actually killing patients by refusing to wash their hands of infectious bacteria before performing an operation, was eventually committed to a mental hospital because of the vicious attacks he received. Galileo, Copernicus, and Joan of Arc were dismissed (or even murdered) as heretics, charlatans, or frauds for having the gall to suggest that reality wasn't structured the way it was originally believed.

The trajectories of many of our field's original thinkers are characterized by less than enthusiastic responses to their introduction of novel ideas to help people. Carl Rogers felt so marginalized by his colleagues and attacked by critics that he fled academic life to start his own institute that would insulate him against continued assaults on his integrity and radical ideas that the helping relationship was in fact at the core of most effective efforts.

The secret of innovation—in any discipline or context—is experimenting, taking risks, trying things that perhaps have never been attempted previously. Thus, initial failure is likely, mistakes are inevitable, and criticism is a certainty, especially from those whose personal interests may be jeopardized by some advance that renders what they are already doing irrelevant, unnecessary, or simply obsolete. It takes courage and tenacity, even in the face of unrelenting attacks, to continue moving forward with ideas or innovations that are not exactly embraced by others.

Chutzpah is derived from both Yiddish and Hebrew to refer to audacity or courage, the willingness to challenge the status quo. This can get out of hand of course, especially when someone's narcissism and blinders lead him or her to blithely proceed forward, leaving innumerable casualties in his or her wake. Humorist Leo Rosten mentioned a classic example of this in a man who murdered his mother and father and then threw himself on the mercy of the court when he became an orphan. *That* is chutzpah.

In the context of our discussion, however, I'm referring to this trait as exemplary of the kind of courage it takes to advance our knowledge and understanding, not by following patterns long established but rather by thinking through what really matters most and trying out new strategies that might very well be groundbreaking. Naturally these efforts are carefully conceived, cautiously implemented, and tested empirically with clear evidence. Chutzpah doesn't mean reckless risk taking but rather passionate, charismatic devotion to seeking truth and greater effectiveness in all areas of life.

The Food Chain

Among most creatures on the planet, there is a distinct hierarchy of status and power depending on one's position within the herd, brood, nest, colony, or tribe. There are alphas and their followers; queens and their workers; and designated leaders who are offered (or take for themselves) a greater share of resources, access to mates, and authority within the group. Sometimes this is based on physical characteristics (strength, size, perceived attractiveness), certain valuable skills (food gathering, healing, navigation, fighting), or age and maturity (with accompanying wisdom), or it is achieved through heroic accomplishments such as public speaking or publication of books or one's reputation among one's peers. Nevertheless, like every other profession, counseling has its luminaries who have attained their positions through legitimate contributions—or sometimes simply self-promotion and self-aggrandizement. This leads to class differences in which we hold that some among us are more important than others. Moreover, it takes a certain chutzpah to challenge the alphas, who enjoy their status and hardly wish to be dethroned by some new kid on the block.

I must admit that I am among those who have struggled with this dynamic even though I may sometimes be regarded among those who have achieved a certain eminence—or at least notoriety. I remember quite vividly being a newcomer to the field, insecure, unworthy, diffident, intimidated by the masters, who struck me as wizards, capable of feats of magic and miracles that would forever be beyond me. But I so desperately wanted to be seen by them, acknowledged, perhaps even someday valued. I think it was this level of desperation that fueled my own chutzpah. I used to routinely write famous authors to ask whether they wanted to coauthor a project with me. I would determinedly seek out those whom I thought were most knowledgeable, and I would not accept no for answer if they rejected my overtures. I surrounded myself with others who shared this life philosophy. One of my friends, Brad Keeney, once showed up at the home of Gregory Bateson (one of the founders of cybernetics and family systems theory) demanding that he be taken on as a student. Other friends, Steve Lankton, Bill O'Hanlon, and Jeff Zeig, did much the same with Milton Erickson.

Bill O'Hanlon, one of the founders of solution-focused counseling, once shared the story of first meeting Erickson when he was a student and asking whether he could study with him. Instead, Erickson hired him as his gardener until such time that O'Hanlon demonstrated sufficient perseverance.

Another favorite story was shared by Steve Lankton, responsible for developing deeper understanding of metaphoric communication and language. He had also traveled to visit Erickson and attend one of his seminars at great expense and sacrifice. Lankton dutifully prepared to learn more advanced forms of hypnotic induction, but Erickson instead sent him out in the desert on a quest to find a mystical object in order to demonstrate his commitment to learning and experimentation. This sort of chutzpah was absolutely seminal in the development of both of these founders. Neither of them actually understood the intended purpose and meaning of these trials, but these experiences helped them to form their own greater willingness to try new things, experiment, and take risks.

Lankton mentioned examples of this lesson learned when describing several of his own cases, in which he asked certain clients to complete seemingly nonsensical tasks that appeared completely unrelated to their presenting complaints. After decades of reflection, he had concluded that Milton Erickson, the great master, sometimes had no idea what he was asking people do, nor could he really articulate a reason other than to stir things up. Lankton realized that this was the method to the apparent madness: It wasn't necessary for the counselor to understand the purpose of a therapeutic assignment as long as it was slightly relevant to the complaint and the client could be invited to create or find the meaning in the experience. This became a guiding principle for his own work helping people initiate safe, constructive risks that lead to changes in behavior that would likely not occur through talk alone.

These are the kinds of stories that inspired me at an early age, stories of adventurers, scientists, or writers who challenged the status quo. They inspired me in such a way that I felt emboldened to test my own capacity for chutzpah. I remember that as an undergraduate studying psychology, I was required to take a class on learning and memory. One of the questions on my take-home exam was to describe B. F. Skinner's theory of forgetting. I looked everywhere in my notes and text for clues, but it struck me that it had to be more complicated than mere extinction. So I looked up ol' B. F.'s (if that's what people called him) phone number, and sure enough it was in the directory in Cambridge, Massachusetts. I dialed his number and a woman answered the phone.

"May I speak to Dr. Skinner please?"

"Sorry," the voice said. "He's not home." I could hear a loud noise in the background that sounded suspiciously like a vacuum cleaner.

"And," I audaciously asked, "who might I ask are you?"

"The housekeeper."

Hmmm. That caught me unprepared. "I have a question for you," I persisted. "By any chance, do you know what Dr. Skinner's theory of forgetting might be?" I knew this was hopeless, but now I was committed.

"No, sorry," she answered and then hung up on me.

Rather than feeling disappointed, I was really quite elated. This was a turning point for me, a door that opened into a world I didn't know that I had access to. It seemed to me, in that moment, that it was entirely possible to at least try to reach out to almost anyone—the worst they could do was decline or not respond at all. My first book proposal was rejected by more than 50 publishers, and I literally used the rejection letters for wallpaper because I was so proud of my persistence.

Jon Carlson discovered a similar phenomenon relatively early in his career when he was a student studying Lawrence Kohlberg's theory of moral development. He had been fascinated by how these ideas of higher order thinking might be applied to help children make better choices and decisions in their lives. Unlike my experience, Carlson actually managed to get Kohlberg to answer his office phone. "Once I described what I had in mind," he recalled, "the great man responded graciously, inviting me to come and visit the following week to attend one of his seminars. I actually did so and it changed everything for me. I realized that there were so many doors that appeared closed to me but they were really negotiable if only I had the chutzpah to knock persistently."

Michael Hoyt describes still another example when he was working on his master's thesis and decided, audaciously, to send it directly to Anna Freud for comments and reactions. Of course he never expected to receive a response and so was surprised when several months later there was a letter in his box with Freud's return address. At the time, Hoyt had been feeling so disheartened with his classes, skipping most of them to hang out at the beach, play Frisbee, and spend time with his girlfriend. Once he opened the envelope, he found a letter that encouraged him in a way that nothing else had done; it became a lifelong secret strategy to reach out to others who interested him most. Sure enough, one of his heroines, the great Anna Freud, had taken the time to write him back, support the research he was doing, and even recommend a journal to which he might send his paper for publication.

"There might be a lot of people higher up on the food chain than I am," Hoyt mentions modestly, "but I've found that if you have the gumption, the chutzpah, to approach 'famous' people, many of them often appreciate being engaged in that way."

What I might add to that observation is not nearly as optimistic. I've found that in fact most of the time busy people seem too busy to respond, which is certainly frustrating, but I've rarely let these disappointments discourage me. I now realize that those whom I like and respect the most consider it a priority in their lives to respond respectfully (and expeditiously) to overtures from others, regardless of their stature and standing.

Going Beyond What Is Convenient and Familiar

There is another kind of courage that has less to do with self-serving motives for advancing one's career and more to do with showing initiative to help others way beyond what might be expected. Conducting counseling sessions in a comfortable office—or even crowded corner—is certainly important, but our profession is also committed to what Alfred Adler referred to as "social interest." For me this has meant not only initiating projects with refugees, trauma survivors, abandoned children, the homeless, and girls at risk for being trafficked into slavery but at times putting my welfare and safety at risk when working in regions that were recovering from earthquakes, disease, civil war, and civil chaos.

Miguel Gallardo believes that it is not chutzpah but rather our moral obligation to stand up for those without power. He has been particularly concerned about the underserved populations within the Latino/a community who don't access counseling services in part because they don't feel that the current mental health delivery system, including those providers who are unaware of what they bring to the room could ever understand or help them. He particularly takes issue with those among us who might take the time to learn a few techniques or strategies but still don't understand the mindset. "Are you comfortable talking about racism, systemic oppression, and have you spent the time understanding what macrosystemic messages your clients endure on a daily basis?" Gallardo asks, challenging the notion that we should remain neutral. "We know that clients who feel understood by their counselors, even when they have not shared the same experiences, drop out less frequently. It has also been shown that clients whose counselor addresses and creates the space for clients to talk about their racist experiences and oppression are less likely to drop out of counseling."

It turns out that chutzpah, that tendency and willingness to be assertive and initiating, must also be balanced with a level of humility and modesty. Gallardo says it best: "I have prioritized serving people, those most in need, and have spent the time walking with humility and being okay with not knowing a whole lot. I have always seen every relationship as an encounter with knowledge, regardless of who I am talking to. My learning never stops, in fact: The more I learn, the more I realize how much I do not know. Our work must privilege the people we serve over theory, the people we serve over policies and performance, and the people we serve over bells and whistles."

As originally utilized, a perso with *chutzpah* was cheeky, bold, fearless, audacious, even overbearing in crossing conventional boundaries or asking for something that was beyond reasonable. There's the story of the old woman selling pretzels on the street for a dollar, her meager stand located outside a high-rise office building downtown. Each day, like clockwork, a well-dressed man in a suit would leave the building exactly at noon, give the woman a dollar as he passed by, but refuse to take a pretzel. This went on for more than 2 years. Monday through Friday, exactly at noon. Then one day, as the man bent over to hand her the money, she withdrew her hand. "Sir," she said, "you've been a very good customer over the years. And I really appreciate your business. But the price of a pretzel is now two dollars."

Personal and Professional Development

Sometimes it is not only our job but our responsibility to ask more from ourselves and from others in order to go beyond the ordinary to produce exceptional outcomes. We can't only depend on mentors and prominent figures (as well as supervisors) to lead us but must take responsibility for our own personal and professional development in order to better serve our clients.

Such self-supervision begins with the awareness that there are so many ways we could be doing better. This means listening to our clients very carefully, responding to their feedback, but also listening to and observing more closely ourselves. I know counselors who are constantly spending idle time reviewing video demonstrations of the masters, systematically studying and decoding their secrets. Even more impressive are those who apply such dedicated self-scrutiny to their own recordings, making notes on ways they could improve their skills. This means of course that they are willing to admit when they feel lost and acknowledge when they have missed something significant. Over time this leads to the most important self-corrective skill of all—which is the ability to recognize problems *as they are occurring in the moment*.

It is just as important to monitor carefully all that is going on inside our minds, watching for internal noise that may be distracting. This also includes constantly recognizing and challenging some of our assumptions that may lead to biases or cognitive errors. It takes considerable practice indeed to distinguish between irrelevant chatter, inappropriate distortions, and revealing insights.

The intersection between personal and professional development is based on the idea that we will never ever be good enough, as good as our clients deserve. This leads us to avoid settling for what we might already do well and instead strive for so much more, just as we teach our clients. This sounds good in theory, but it is actually quite difficult to give up what is already familiar in order to discover something altogether new and likely awkward to apply right away.

Another important secret of exceptional counselors is that they remind themselves constantly of the incredible joys and benefits of their professional work and all the ways they enhance their personal functioning. Those among us who feel discouraged, or who operate on autopilot, may complain a lot about being unappreciated, overworked, and underpaid. They focus altogether too much on their burdens rather than the privileges of being a counselor. Yes, this is incredibly hard work that can be so challenging in a number of ways. But amazing gifts come our way, some of which we have come to take for granted:

- Altruism: feeling (perhaps knowing) that we are making a constructive difference in people's lives
- Intimacy: enjoying incredible closeness to others in such meaningful relationships
- Learning: increasing knowledge and awareness of the human experience on so many levels
- Drama: experiencing the drama and excitement and intensity of others' crises and transitions
- Stories: hearing the seminal and meaningful narratives of people's most private lives
- Challenges: experimenting and trying out new ways of interacting with others in order to promote breakthroughs

Perhaps most of all, the trait of chutzpah, the courage of risk taking, helps us to become not only more inventive and proactive in our therapeutic interventions but also far more reflective about our own life journey. Regardless of our theoretical allegiances and professional styles, each of us discovers the secret of being more contemplative, analytic, and intuitive as a way of being in all facets of our existence.

CHAPTER 11

Clients Lie—a Lot—and It Might Not Matter

Although we often talk about the importance of trust in the counseling relationship, it is usually in the context of helping clients to trust *us,* not with respect to how it is also important for us to trust *them.* It isn't exactly a secret that clients are often less than perfectly honest and forthcoming about all the things going on in their lives. Nevertheless, it's still somewhat puzzling why people would deliberately obfuscate or deceive the very professionals they have hired to help them. Actually, it's not all that surprising considering how important it is to them that we like and approve of them. And then there's the issue of how powerful it feels to be able to fool an expert who is supposedly a know-it-all.

There have been times when each of us has been spectacularly duped by clients who went *way* beyond the usual standards of duplicity. It wasn't just a matter of embellishing their job responsibilities, minimizing how often they drank, glossing over a few significant details, or even exaggerating symptoms but also creating a whole fantasy persona that appeared in the room.

I previously had no interest in this subject, given that I prefer to believe almost anything that a client tells me, not because I'm naïve or gullible but because I don't like to operate from a position of suspicion and doubt. Once it becomes evident that things are not exactly as portrayed, there are often ways to adjust this new information in such a way that clients don't feel shamed for being less than honest. After all, on one level you'd have to be crazy to just open up and tell your deepest, darkest secrets to a perfect stranger.

I had been approached by an elderly man who was obviously suffering from symptoms of trauma from earlier in his life. Once his story unfolded, it was revealed that he had served in a brutal war as a kind of special forces operative whose job was to assassinate enemy leaders. We worked together for more than a year, during which time he described some of the violent missions he'd been required to complete, killing people at close range, working behind enemy lines, eventually being captured and tortured before a daring rescue freed him. This was the first time he had ever told anyone about this secret life, and he was irrationally terrified that certain "authorities" might discover that he'd confessed his "crimes." When pressed, he explained that he'd been told that his missions were so secret and off the books that if they were discovered there would be "serious repercussions." That seemed to imply that he might be erased, just as the records had been expunged.

It felt like I was living inside a spy novel whenever he would show up for his customary Wednesday morning appointment. Each session was filled with drama and the kind of thrilling action stories that one usually found in movies. But this was *real,* and I was like a panting dog waiting for the next installment.

It was only later, *much* later than I'd like to admit, that I began to question whether any of this had really happened and whether he really was who he said he was. Some of the pieces didn't quite fit together. I started to remember that when I would press for details about some of his alleged escapades, he was less than forthcoming. Eventually I became convinced that he had made up most of this fictitious biography to entertain himself, to hook and play with me, or perhaps because he was just a sad old man who was simply sharing the kind of life he wished he had led.

But no, this story is not yet over. A few years later, after the man died, his wife called me to tell me that he'd left me a letter. My hands were shaking when I opened up the envelope, thinking that now I would finally hear his honest confession and perhaps an apology for playing with me. That was not to be. Instead, his letter acknowledged that he knew that I was skeptical about what he'd shared with me but he wanted me to know that in spite of his faulty and aged memory, most of what he could remember he'd told me was indeed the absolute truth. If anything, there was a lot more that he had never gotten around to telling me.

It's many years later and I *still* don't know what to believe. I honestly don't know whether the man really had been a secret agent assassin in a previous life and was suffering from guilt and trauma after his violent deeds or whether he had made the whole thing up. But it got me thinking: How do we know that anything our clients tell us is true? And how much does it matter?

What to Believe?

It makes sense that clients would wish to hide. They would want to bide their time until they could be certain that their counselor is truly safe. In some cases, it doesn't feel like they are really lying at all because they actually believe some of the ridiculous things they are spouting out loud:

- "What do you mean? Of *course* I had a happy childhood!"
- "Oh. I didn't really think telling you about that was important."
- "These problems are really not my fault. It's just that other people just don't get me."

- "Yeah I drink. Everyone does. But it's not really a problem."
- "Oh, sorry about that. I guess I sort of forgot."
- "Yeah, that makes sense."

We understand that being honest is difficult, especially about things that spark shame. We get that. But it doesn't explain the extent to which some people will go so far out of their way to make our jobs so much more difficult than they need to be. We take at face value that a client proclaims that he is miserable and wants to change. We choose to believe the stories our clients bring to us, at least until such time as they are clearly fictionalizations. And even then we might not choose to confront such doubts. After all, if the client believes that something is true, maybe that is an alternative reality.

In a previous project, I interviewed dozens of counselors and asked them to tell me about their own experiences with deception in counseling. I found it both pretty disturbing as well as hilarious the extent to which some clients would fib even if it was just sabotaging their own progress. One client pretended to have a degenerative disease that confined her to a wheelchair, that is until she was spotted walking around town one day. Another claimed she was dying of cancer when she was actually perfectly healthy. Even more interesting is that one client failed to show for an appointment one day, and when the counselor called to find out what happened, he was informed that the client had just died of cancer. The intriguing part, however, is that even after a year of weekly sessions, this client had never once mentioned that he was struggling with a terminal disease.

Some of the cases mentioned are far more disturbing. A client scheduled an appointment at the counseling center on campus because of severe depression and suicidal ideation. The counselor assigned to the student's case conducted a thorough intake focused in particular on an assessment of potential self-harm, coping mechanisms, support system, and other critical factors. Everything appeared to be going well during the interview until the client walked out the door and muttered under his breath that he may not return for another appointment because he might not be around any longer. Then he disappeared.

It took the counselor a few moments to process what happened and what his final words had meant. Was he saying that he was dropping out of school? Or was this a genuine suicide threat? Was he saying goodbye? The counselor didn't quite know what to make of the comment and whether it required her to take decisive action. Should she notify authorities? Was it time to commit him to inpatient care? She worried all week about the young man, frequently second-guessing herself.

When the student showed up for his next appointment on time, she breathed a sigh of relief. "I'm so glad to see you," she said, a bit more enthusiastically than she intended. She didn't want him to know how much time she had spent thinking about him.

"Yeah, about that," he said, standing up in the doorway but not taking the customary chair. "I'm not here for counseling."

"Excuse me?"

"I said I didn't come for counseling."

"No? I'm confused. Then why are you here?" She was puzzled about why he was grinning at her as he was telling her this.

"Yeah, you see, I'm really an acting student. And I was just messing with you to see if I could fool you." With that, he twiddled his fingers at her and walked away.

Counselors confided other instances in which particular clients played with them, even pretended to be someone entirely different. One client sat in the waiting room and would pretend to be a counselor in the clinic and encourage others to disclose why they were there. Another client swiped his counselor's wallet and began impersonating him. And perhaps one of the most extreme examples is a client who claimed to be an arson investigator for the state attorney's office. He regularly showed up at crime scenes and consulted on cases, even making significant contributions studying forensic evidence. He finally got caught, and the counselor was so notified, when the fire department called the state attorney's office to thank them for sending their investigator. The problem of course was that they'd never heard of him.

Such cases are admittedly pretty rare. Most of the time, the so-called truth eventually comes out once trust is fully established within the relationship. And frankly, except for really extreme cases such as those mentioned above, I wonder how much it really matters whether clients are being completely open and honest or not. On the one hand, we work with whatever clients bring into the room, and that doesn't necessarily mean that it must be a fully accurate portrayal of their experience. After all, I have witnessed some pretty incredible trauma treatments in which clients never even talked out loud about the actual incidents and instead did the work inside their own heads.

On the other hand—and of course there *is* another perspective—it certainly does matter at times whether a client is being truthful. I was taught that no matter what the client says, you basically accept it as truth, or at least *his or her* truth. I was told that if I act as if I believe the client, that's how I will be able to best maintain a solid relationship. The client will feel trusted and comfortable sharing deeper, more personal issues. I was also taught that if I told clients that I don't believe their stories, I might be right, but the counseling, for all practical purposes, will stop at that moment. One counselor who does a lot of supervision offered the following rule of thumb that guided him: If you always (or mostly) choose to believe what your clients say, you might get burned 1 out of 10 times. But if you take a skeptical position and choose not to believe them, you will get burned *every* time.

One counselor shared a very unusual approach to working with his clients. He didn't feel that it was necessary for them to share many details of what was most bothersome because he preferred to work with them inside their own heads rather than saying everything out loud. Clients avoided the temptation to distort or lie because it wasn't considered important to reveal things that were uncomfortable: "I want you to imagine that you are still stuck in that situation that terrifies you so much. Now signal me when you are *there,* when you feel it most strongly. Okay, now I want you to imagine that you have other resources and ways you might respond differently than you have previously. I want you . . ."

You get the point. When using imagery, mindfulness exercises, or what has been called the *skeleton key, looking for exceptions, unique outcomes,* and a bunch of other names depending on the theory, the goal is to allow clients to work at their own pace and within their own internal world. Sometimes catharsis, or sharing things out loud, isn't all that helpful, as we've discovered with more current research on traumatic stress debriefing and other intrusive methods.

The key secret that most exceptional counselors have discovered is that it isn't always useful or even necessary to directly confront a client who is not being altogether truthful or accurate. Sometimes it is best to allow people to keep their illusions, and especially their dignity, rather than calling them out just to satisfy our own needs.

When to Challenge, When to Question, When to Wait

When Richard first came to counseling, he immediately began complaining about how he was being singled out, picked on, and never considered for promotion. He thought that this was totally unfair because he was the best salesperson in the car dealership and had the largest number of returning customers. "Last week," he boasted, "I even sold a car that had been on the lot for almost a year!" Then he held out his hands, as if to invite agreement.

The counselor listened carefully as Richard continued talking about how successful he was and yet how unappreciated he felt by his colleagues and bosses. The counselor in turn felt himself becoming increasingly annoyed and suspicious that this situation could possibly be as described. He'd only known Richard for a few minutes and already felt turned off by his excessive boasting and self-promotion. No wonder he was having problems at work and likely in other areas of his life. The counselor thought about challenging him, pointing out this poor-me attitude that focused on blaming everyone else for his problems. Instead, he took a deep breath and waited a bit until finally he could wait no longer.

"Richard, stop for a moment if you don't mind."

"What?" he abruptly replied, obviously unhappy with the interruption.

"I was just wondering: Who else sees this situation the same way that you do?"

"I don't understand," Richard said. "What are you saying? You don't believe me? How *else* could anyone see this? I'm just describing what happened." Then he crossed his arms and sat back.

"Well," the counselor continued in a softer voice, "I guess what I'm asking is whether others believe that you are so much better than the other sales staff at the showroom and that everyone else is being unfair to you?"

There was a long pause at this point, and the counselor wondered whether he had gone too far. Finally, Richard shook his head. "Well, they probably wouldn't agree because they're just jealous."

"You mean everyone else at work, all your peers as well as your supervisors?" The counselor wasn't going to let him off the hook too easily.

Richard nodded, very reluctantly.

"I'm wondering then if there might be another way to look at things?"

"What do you mean?"

"I'm just suggesting there might be another way to view your situation, one that may reveal some other reasons why you keep encountering difficulties and feel so unappreciated. It seems this has happened to you several times before."

"I'm not sure . . . I mean, I don't know . . . I try to get along with everyone, show them what to do, given them advice and stuff."

"And do they appreciate your help in this way?"

"Well, no, but maybe they . . ."

"So you keep trying to help others but you do it in such a way that they don't feel inclined to accept what you are offering? That's kind of puzzling, isn't it?"

"I guess so."

"And you've said something similar about why your girlfriend gets mad at you and why your brother won't talk to you anymore."

Here's an example in which the client is not so much trying to deceive the counselor as simply engaging in a little image management. It's important to Richard that his counselor is on his side. If he is not altogether accurate in presenting the situation, it is because he is protecting himself through *self*-deception, the most common form of deception that we encounter every day.

Yet as mentioned, the secret of experienced counselors is to avoid, when possible, directly challenging or confronting clients when we sense that they are not being totally forthcoming or honest—at least until such time that the relationship can withstand such potentially threatening conversations. In this example, the counselor instead tries to adopt a more inquisitive posture, asking questions that give Richard space to maneuver if he doesn't yet feel ready to tackle the issues that have been uncovered.

The Meanings of Deception

One interesting question related to this discussion, one that I've been musing about for some time, is how much it matters the extent to which the client is telling the unvarnished truth, so to speak. We always expect some level of distortion, exaggeration, minimization, denial, and fibbing, perhaps in *any* conversation, especially considering that almost every conversation that lasts more than 10 minutes contains at least two lies. To some degree, it certainly matters how accurate clients are in reporting what actually happened and how they responded, but then that brings up the whole idea of constructed realities: If a client genuinely believes that a certain thing happened in a particular way, then perhaps that is just a different kind of reality, one that exerts just as much influence as events are remembered.

A key feature of any level of deceit is the actual intention and motive behind the behavior, which sparks a number of intriguing questions. Is the client fudging the truth because he or she fears judgment? Does it signal compromised trust in the relationship? Does the reluctance demonstrate feelings of shame and guilt, or perhaps just uncertainty? How much difference does it make whether the client is knowingly leading you astray versus inadvertently doing so? What about the distinctions between clients who might lie to protect themselves in some way and those who deliberately deceive as a demonstration of their power? And one final question: What about the times when *we* might deceive or shade the truth, feeling justified that it's in the client's best interests?

There are so many reasons why a client may be deceptive or engage in chronic deceit. Most commonly, such behavior may reflect a fear of shame and humiliation or perhaps concerns about disappointing the counselor. It can also represent a test for trust. Certainly we have also encountered individuals who simply lie for a living, so to speak. They might be described, diagnostically speaking, as sociopathic, borderline, or histrionic or have other personality disturbances that feature manipulation and deception. Then there are also conditions such as Ganzer syndrome, Munchausen syndrome, Korsakov syndrome, factitious disorders, or memory impairments that lead to making up stories. I even came across an obscure condition called *pseudologica fantastica* in which clients create a self-aggrandizing story that they come to believe is actually true. Finally, there are psychotic distortions in which one's fantasies become an alternative reality. To someone with symptoms of schizophrenia, it may very well be real that he has been captured by aliens, that he has been pursued by foreign spies, or that poisonous spiders are living inside his bowels.

When clients were asked directly about the reasons why they lied to their counselors, even when it seemed to sabotage progress they could make in sessions, they often said something like the following:

- "I don't yet trust my counselor, partly because I'm not confident that he has the skills or experience to handle my problems in the first place."
- "I lie to my counselor about what I'm feeling toward her. I'm embarrassed about these feelings, and when I do try to share them, they come out wrong. I know I'm already too dependent. I want more than what she can give me, so I try to control that by not being truthful."
- "We all lie to our shrinks, just like we lie to our dentists (Sure, I'll floss twice a day.) But the point of repeat visits to our shrinks is to allow for the time necessary to figure out what's a lie, what's a misconception, and what the truth (for that day) is."

We must also accept ourselves as flawed beings, prone to the same kinds of defenses, difficulties, and distortions as anyone else. Of course we protect ourselves by trying to look on the bright side of things and minimize whatever is uncomfortable or unresolved. Of course we may lie to ourselves—and others—on occasion. Sometimes we do this to protect others, so they don't feel hurt or rejected: "Of *course* I like you! You are one of my favorite clients, and I so look forward to our conversations."

Dark Secrets

Thus far I have been presenting secrets in the context of unheralded ideas and strategies that counselors and therapists have found to be most helpful. But there are other secrets that we hold and rarely talk about. I have discussed many of them in earlier works, but it is worth reviewing some of them once again, especially those that are most universal even if they are rarely discussed.

- *"I'm not really listening."* There are many, many times (more than we would ever admit) when we sit in sessions, nodding our heads, inserting a few "uh huhs," but thinking about something altogether different from what is being said: what we are going to make for dinner, who the client reminds us of, whether to head straight home after work or stop to see a friend. We pretend to pay attention when we are actually a thousand miles away.
- *"When I am listening, I'm actually being very critical."* As much as I might try to still the judgmental voice in my head, it rears its ugly head at the most inopportune times. "That's the dumbest thing I've ever heard." "No wonder you can't make a relationship last; I can barely survive an hour with you each week." "Sometimes I wish I could just knock some sense into you when you spout that crap."
- *"I don't understand what's going on."* This is the norm. If we are honest with ourselves, much of the time we are confused and uncertain about what is really going on. Although we live constantly with this ambiguity and complexity, the stress is magnified by the expectation that we are supposed to pretend a level of confidence that is way beyond what is reasonable.
- *"I don't really know what I'm doing."* This corollary of the dark secret just mentioned refers more to our hesitant actions than the ways we try to make sense of things. No matter which intervention we try, which therapeutic skill we bring to bear, how we might frame an interpretation or reflection, which metaphor or story we introduce, there are so many other, different, perhaps better choices we could have made instead.

  We aren't exactly sure what happened or why. It's not really that we don't know what we are doing—because we do. It's just that whichever course of action we initiate we must also consider that there isn't a clear way to determine whether it was best—no matter what clients report or how enthusiastically they say they are better. (Remember, they lie.)

- *"I don't really know if my client is better or not."* Even when we think we know what's going on and feel assured that we are headed in the best direction, it's still disconcerting that we can't really ever know for sure whether a client is actually improving. Milton Erickson once remarked that even if our clients are just pretending to change, if they pretend long and hard enough, over time they will come to believe that the transformation is real.
- *"I'm a hypocrite."* This is the most disturbing lie of all, one that is entitled to its own chapter. We don't always practice what we preach to others. We ask people to do things we are unable—or unwilling—to do ourselves. We admonish clients to take charge of their lives while we remain complacent in our own. We urge them to take risks while we play it safe. We motivate them to experiment with new ways of being even though we might remain mired in predictable patterns. We behave compassionately, sensitively, supportively when the meter is running during sessions but have been known to lash out at others we care the most about. In all kinds of ways, we say one thing but do quite another when we think nobody is watching.

This. Is. Not. Acceptable.

CHAPTER 12

Techniques Sometimes Matter

During his prime, the late composer, producer, and musical innovationist Prince mastered more than a dozen different instruments, including the guitar and bass, saxophone, harmonica, various percussions, and keyboard. On one composition, *For You,* he arranged every one of the 27 instruments featured on the album. Like many exceptional artists and practitioners, Prince mastered a variety of different styles and techniques depending on what he felt was most appropriate for any given situation.

Similarly, exceptional counselors have within their repertoire an extraordinary number of choices they can make in response to any given clinical moment. Whether in the form of interventions, techniques, or behavior, they can do a multitude of different things depending on what is required.

"I just don't know what to do with my daughter," Teresa begins, explaining why she is seeking help. "Krista is 17 but she, I don't know, she acts like a child."

The counselor nods, encouraging her to continue.

"She just isn't doing what she's capable of doing. She has so much potential, but . . ." Teresa just shrugs.

"So tell me what that's like for you," the counselor prompts.

"Well, it just seems the more I try to help her, the less she does. It's just so damn . . ."

". . . frustrating," the counselor finishes.

"Yeah. And my husband, Fred, isn't much better. They're like two peas in a pod. I'm sure that's where she got it from."

"Krista and your husband are a lot alike," the counselor repeats, still buying some time to figure out the landscape.

"You got that right for sure. Fred, he's a nice guy and all, and we get along pretty well. We've been married, what, 20 years, on and off." She laughs as she says that, leaving the counselor to wonder about whether they were separated at times.

"But Fred, I don't know, he just doesn't seem to have any gumption."

"You mean he doesn't have a lot of ambition the way that you do?"

"Yeah, I guess that's it."

"So you feel alone a lot, as if the two of them have formed a kind of alliance against you."

Teresa nods and tears start forming.

It's at this juncture that the counselor, relying almost exclusively on simple reflections, is exploring some of what is going on. Of course before trying any intervention, he conducts a basic assessment of the situation.

"Tell me, Teresa, given how lonely and isolated you feel and your frustration with your daughter and husband, how do you cope?"

"I guess I drink a little. Maybe sometimes more than a little."

"Uh huh. What else?"

"Smoke some weed?"

"You get high sometimes? How often?"

"What do you mean?"

"How often do you smoke marijuana or drink alcohol?"

"Oh," she giggles, "just about every chance I can get."

It turns out that Teresa relies on alcohol or marijuana as a primary coping strategy, although now there is some collateral damage. She is terrified that mandatory drug testing at work will reveal the extent of her addictions and she'll lose her job. Given that Fred and Krista aren't contributing much to the family income, she feels that most of the responsibility to support everyone is falling on her shoulders. She explains that Fred is in real estate but hasn't sold a house in several months.

"Wow," the counselor responds, "that's a lot of pressure on you."

"If you only knew," she says, head bowed down, hands squeezed tight. "Besides, I hate my damn job. I have to get up at 5:30 every morning. It takes over an hour in traffic to get there, and my boss is the biggest asshole you'd ever want to meet."

This is only a small slice of the picture of Teresa's life. During this initial session, she also discloses that their house is falling apart and they're behind in their mortgage payments, even in danger of default. Her eldest son, who moved out a few months ago, is living with a girl whom Teresa believes is a complete loser. "Supposedly they're both going to move to Florida and become professional surfers or some damn thing."

Okay, this is *your* case. Where do you begin? What do you see as the best focus of counseling? What would you identify as the main issue or problem? What strategies might you use to help this client?

It's always interesting to hear different perspectives on how a variety of counselors might conceptualize a case and work with a particular client. There is *so* much here to work with that I imagine an assortment of practitioners might approach this case from all kinds of viewpoints and conceptual paradigms. Even among those who share the same model, very different therapeutic pathways would likely be articulated and implemented.

I asked Jon Carlson, a noted Adlerian theorist, what he might do with this client. "It's so easy to become overwhelmed with a case like this, especially when we get into empathy mode, looking at things through the client's eyes," he said. Carlson preferred to keep himself grounded by reminding himself of the three main tasks of life that Adler first articulated: work, love, and friendships. When applied to Teresa's situation, it helped him organize and center on what might be the optimal priorities. Counselors using other models will naturally follow alternative routes, perhaps examining gender scripts that limit Teresa, family systems ideas that help explain the dysfunctional interaction dynamics, self-talk that sabotages constructive action, internalized narratives, and so on. In each case, the model both suggests a choice of interventions as well as limits other choices.

Carlson would systematically examine and address each of the areas previously mentioned. "My secret strategy, internalized long ago from my early Adler training, is first to acknowledge to the client how overwhelmed I feel by everything she shared, so I can't imagine what it must be like for her. I'd suggest we both take a deep breath and review each of the three areas of concern. Let's start with work."

Teresa might then be encouraged to talk about the aspects of her job she does enjoy rather than just the difficulties she experiences with her supervisor. She admits that it isn't the job itself that is the problem so much as the excessive burden of responsibility she feels to support the family. She also would like to find work closer to home so she doesn't spend so much time stuck in traffic, another source of stress for her.

Next Carlson would hone in on her love life, which is not going well at all because of the resentment she feels toward her husband for not carrying his share of their financial responsibility. "I love the guy, I really do," she says with a smile. "I miss our closeness. But I just get so angry at him sometimes when it seems like he's just sitting around feeling sorry for himself. I guess that's why I have so little patience with my daughter as well."

"And as far as your social life?" Carlson would ask. "Your friends and support system?"

"Down the toilet."

"Excuse me?"

"I just don't have the time or the energy. I miss my friends of course. But it just feels like one more thing I have to do. When I get home I just want to crash."

After reviewing each of these areas of life, Carlson would next ask what might help in any of them that she'd like to tackle first. "When clients come to counseling," Carlson explained, "they nearly always come because of difficulty with one or more of these life tasks. The difficulties arise from inaccuracies, mistakes, and maladaptive perceptions associated with their style of life. Therefore, the overarching counseling goal is to help clients adjust or modify their style of life in ways that help them address these critical areas."

The More the Better?

Whereas Carlson preferred to work from within a flexible Adlerian perspective that allowed him to draw from those signature techniques, Philip

Kirk, a counselor in private practice, keeps adding to his therapeutic options, the more the better. Kirk is a big fan of the kinds of techniques that consistently lead clients to become more invested in their sessions. He also recognizes that all techniques are contextual, are situational, and must be personalized for any client and issue.

Kirk isn't sure that his favorite techniques are much of a secret, believing that it isn't necessary to invent something new so much as adapt it as you might any tool that doesn't quite fit the task. One example he points to is the use of cognitive schemas, those internal messages that limit possibilities and reinforce a negative self-image. "We have all worked with clients who make excuses and build barriers to justify their immobility. These same clients want a validation that gives them a pass that it is okay to remain stuck."

Whether the technique is called *spitting in the client's soup* or *a bitter pill to swallow,* Kirk finds it invaluable to confront his clients in the most nonthreatening way possible, suggesting, "Could it be . . .?" or "I wonder if . . .?" His secret is to present new or potentially threatening ideas as conceptualizations to be considered and tried on for size.

Mary Schor, a counseling student, interviewed several practitioners about their favorite signature techniques that they developed or adapted themselves based on existing ideas. These were strategies that they personalized to fit their own style and clinical context. Joe, a combat vet, works with returning military personnel experiencing posttraumatic stress. One of his go-to secrets is to use something he calls the *tape recorder technique.* He tells clients that we all have a tape recorder in our minds. We have the ability to rewind to the past and fast-forward to the future, but we ordinarily only rewind or play the tape up to the present moment. He then teaches clients to play their tapes all the way through to the consequences of the actions they are considering. This works particularly well with addicts who are in danger of relapsing and clients who are thinking about cheating on their spouse or partner. When they fully think through the consequences of their actions, they are less likely to engage in self-destructive behavior. Schor found this technique to be particularly interesting because she could imagine all kinds of ways that she might use it with herself, much less with clients.

Schor also interviewed Stephen, an additions counselor whose favorite technique is to ask a client to write down his or her "conditions of satisfaction," a variation of what others might call *looking for exceptions* or *unique outcomes.* Once again, this is an example of a professional who takes existing ideas or methodologies and makes them his own. Stephen appreciates that these satisfactory conditions can actually be measured over time, giving clients a means by which they can continuously assess their progress toward goals.

Not a Technique but a Way of Being With Clients

Although in this chapter and the one that follows there is considerable discussion about specific interventions that certain counselors favor, John

Murphy mentions that his most valuable secret is that our work isn't really about techniques at all. Although he might rely on some strategies that he has found generally useful, they are less about a method and much more about relational engagement. Because he works a lot with children who are apprehensive about counseling in the first place, he likes to find ways to lessen their anxiety and fears. "I often ask them to help me with a simple physical task such as moving a stack of books from one place to another, repositioning a chair, helping me adjust a picture frame so that it's level, and so forth. This is not a technique from a clinical theory or text, but I've found it helpful in giving clients an easy win and beginning the therapeutic relationship on a casual, nonthreatening, successful note."

Murphy finds it interesting that asking his client for help, even with something relatively simple, changes the dynamic of the relationship to make it more collaborative from the outset. "I seek to build with every client the kind of relationship that conveys the idea that I need clients' help in order to be useful to them. I need them to teach me who they are and what they want most from counseling, what I can do to be most effective for them. I also need their ongoing feedback on the fit and outcomes of counseling. This quick little task, as trivial as it may appear, plants the seed for a collaborative alliance in which the client's input and contributions take center stage throughout the change process."

Another counselor has discovered a similar secret that has guided her practice. "I think in the beginning, often times, I was very anxious, tentative, and nervous. I felt like every moment of a session had to be prepared for and planned for, that I had to know what techniques I was going to use." She makes the point that at least in some ways, such preparation and encyclopedic knowledge of theory can sometimes block the best possibilities for progress.

"I think over time," she continues, "you learn the value of sitting back a little bit more, allowing the client to take more responsibility for what goes on. It's about learning to be present, to listen carefully, and often to let go of techniques and interventions." The secret is to eventually find balance between what we think we know, what we believe we understand, what we've stored in our bag of tricks, and what is actually going on in the room in any given moment—just watching and listening with awe and interest.

When It's Time to Do Something

Although I have frequently been reassured that our best work takes place when we stay present and let the client do the work—and have offered that advice to many others—there is a part of me that doesn't believe that is nearly enough. There are times when we must do something fairly decisive, take charge, introduce structure, change direction, or otherwise intervene.

Let's put aside for the moment any specific technique, which will always vary depending on the situation, the client, the issue, the context, and your mood, and instead focus on simply the idea that *something* must usually be done in certain circumstances. Let's take silence in a session as an example. The client has just shared a very disturbing incident that occurred in his childhood, one that seems to imply that there was some possible sexual abuse. How do you respond?

Well naturally there are dozens of things you might do, but you decide to reflect the underlying feeling you sense: "That's been so difficult for you to finally say out loud since it's something you've been wondering about for some time."

Silence goes on for more than a minute (which is a *long* time to sit and wait).

"I can see this is difficult for you to talk about," you try once again. "It's really uncomfortable to go back into the past and dredge this stuff up again."

Once again, silence continues. The client stares down at the floor. Complete stillness.

Now what do you do?

I think we'd all agree that you have to do *something*, even if that something is just to wait. But the technique or response you'd choose would depend very much on what you think the silence means. Is he so flooded he can't talk? Is he reflecting on things and just needs time to process before replying? Is he punishing you for being too intrusive and stirring up these painful memories? Perhaps he is carrying on a dialogue inside his head, rehearsing what he has to say? Or maybe he's just done—he's said all he wants to say and is waiting for you to take the lead and move on to something else. The point here is that often the choice of a specific technique or response is not as important as the reading of the situation and the recognition that one is needed.

I've always found reassurance in the idea that as long as I realize that a response is required, even if I can't settle on what exactly to do, and if I've created a solid enough relationship with the client(s), they will give me the latitude to try a few things until we get something right. Anyway, usually clients are so caught up in their own experience they hardly notice when our first few attempts fall short.

I close with my secret list of a few of those instances when I *know* it's time to do something in a session:

1. It's time to do something when the client is rambling incessantly as a filibuster to prevent us from getting into far more meaningful material. This is sometimes my own impatience and boredom talking, so I have to be particularly careful to sort out whether this is related to my own need to move things along or truly reflects the client's preferred pace.
2. It's time to do something when the sessions have slipped into a predictable routine that may be stifling new and more innovative ways to explore and deal with issues. Once again, this could reflect my own preference for novelty and stimulation, but I also think that it's important to keep things from becoming stale. I'm often unsure how to do that, or what technique is going to move things to a new

and different level, but often the best option is simply to reflect my own experience, assuming it is not self-indulgence: "I sense that we are both getting so used to doing things a particular way that we have hit an impasse. I wonder how we might change our sessions in a way that would be more useful to us?"

3. Most of us are sensitive to language that clients use, either internally or in their conversations. Depending on one's theoretical orientation, this might be called *internal scripts, self-talk, irrational beliefs, alternative storylines, colonized beliefs,* and so on. There are instances in which we observe or hear clients engage in the kinds of self-defining and self-limiting language (exaggerations, distortions, perfectionism, victimization, etc.) that requires some attention. Whether the choice is simply to note the pattern for a more appropriate moment or to confront the behavior vigorously is a matter of circumstance.
4. Much of our work often takes the form of validating, affirming, reinforcing, and supporting constructive or positive behavior—acting as a cheerleader to encourage incremental progress. We look for every opportunity to point out when a client does something well, or at least in the right direction. There are all kinds of variations on techniques that range from the direct ("I'm so proud of you and what you've done") to the indirect (the use of metaphors, paradox, and exaggeration).
5. No matter how relaxed, laid back, or nondirective a counselor might be, there are definite times when structure is needed. A client is floundering, drowning in indecision, lost and confused beyond the point where it can be reasonably tolerated, and some sort of direction is needed. Once again I'm not advocating a particular technique so much as suggesting that some intervention is required, whether that takes the form of (a) taking a time-out to discuss what may be happening, (b) offering an interpretation or explanation, (c) reflecting and acknowledging the feelings that are occurring, (d) moving from talk to action in the form of an enactment or role play, (e) switching gears altogether to a different topic, (f) comforting someone who is feeling incredibly anxious, (g) paradoxically prescribing more and deeper confusion, or (h) rescuing the client by providing clear and detailed structure to once again find stable ground.
6. Perhaps this is just a personal preference, but one of my secrets has always been to block complaining whenever possible. I've usually considered it a colossal waste of time and energy to talk about things that are way beyond one's control. I've worked in crowded, urban areas where clients complain constantly about the traffic. I've worked in northern climates in which clients go on incessantly about how cold it is and in southern climates in which they complain about the heat and humidity. Many clients use their unhappy childhoods as a ready excuse for all the problems that they have. And then there are all the complaints about how unappreciated people feel or how fate, bad luck, or forces of the universe are the reasons why they haven't achieved their goals.

I don't mean to be unsympathetic or intolerant (okay, maybe a little), but there are indeed times when it is appropriate to stop clients from going on and on about things that really are outside of their control, such as politics, the weather, or other such subjects. A certain amount of catharsis and whining can feel good, for a little while, but there is a point when we must often break in and redirect attention to other, more empowering topics.

7. One of our jobs, regardless of orientation and style, is to help people come to terms with behavior that is getting in their way. This is often the result of blind spots that prevent them from making needed changes. Thus, we are often required to call greater attention to inconsistencies and discrepancies between (a) what clients say they want and what they are actually doing, (b) what clients are saying now and something they said earlier, (c) what clients claim is true and evidence of some more objective reality, and (d) what they are saying about themselves and the way we or others experience them. In other words, confrontation is sometimes in order via a variety of techniques. The goal of such interventions is to provide constructive feedback that may ultimately lead to changes in entrenched patterns that are clearly ineffective.

I've reviewed these examples of when an intervention or response is indicated to emphasize that although it's nice to have an assortment of choices available, it's just as important to recognize that timing is critical. Techniques are *always* embedded in relational connections; they are neither effective nor ineffective in and of themselves. And one secret of exceptional counselors is to constantly remind themselves that any specific intentional strategy, intervention, response, skill, or technique is less important than the overall interactive effect that is composed of so many other unseen, unknown, unanticipated factors that also come into play.

CHAPTER 13

More Advanced Techniques That Are Rarely Mentioned

If we consider once again what distinguishes an exceptional counselor from the rest of the pack, one factor might be related to the use of strategies beyond the expertise of most others. As in any craft, there are stages of professional development as we accumulate experience, training, and supervision. A *novice* sticks to the most basic and relatively benign skills and techniques, such as the kinds of reflections, paraphrases, and summary statements that students learn in their first classes. An *initiate* can handle straightforward, simple cases, perhaps sticking to intake interviews and handling a few adjustment reactions. An *apprentice* is considered a member of the guild, an intern who has begun to experiment with more complex and advanced techniques that may take years to master. A *journey(wo)man* has attained a level of competence characterized by about two thirds of practicing counselors. Such clinicians can practice without supervision and attain reasonable effectiveness with most people who walk in the door. An *expert* has extensive experience in multiple domains and is distinguished by a specialized ability to work with even the most challenging cases. Then there is the true *master,* an expert's expert, a professional who has attained elite status as a result of extraordinary excellence across a wide spectrum of areas. Such an individual sets standards or ideals for the profession and can do things that others among us can only watch in awe.

Experience Counts—All Kinds of Experience

Although most of us will never attain a position of true mastery as counselors, considering the kind of extraordinary devotion, commitment, and talent that requires, we can—and do—accumulate valuable experiences in sessions and in daily life that increase the depth of our understanding and add to our repertoire of therapeutic options. One example of this was described by Jon Carlson, who was a practicing Buddhist and meditator throughout his life. He found a way to bring that reflective experience into sessions as a technique to ground and focus himself.

"I find myself centering before each session," he explained. "This centering is now done with a breath and a quick focus on clients before they come into the counseling room." Carlson tried to imagine what it must be like to live in their skin based on what he already knew about them. *How did they get to this place in life?* he would wonder. *What must have happened? How did they learn to be the way they are?*

If Carlson's secret for centering himself before and during sessions used strong doses of mindfulness, he also favored more provocative techniques that took him many years to master without pushing clients too hard and too far. One of these strategies was designed to move clients off their inertia due to fears of failure.

A client might say, for instance, "I've had this problem for so long that I can't remember a time when I ever felt really free from it."

"When were you first aware that this was a problem for you?" Carlson would ask.

"Gee. Um. I don't really know."

"You don't have any idea when you first started having difficulties?" he would press again.

"Not really."

"What about an estimate?"

The client would shrug.

"Take a wild guess."

"I just don't know. I mean it could be . . ."

"Just take a stab at it. Just your best hunch."

A long pause. Then, "Well, I do remember one time when I was about 8 years old and my father came home later than usual. I was in my room. I think I was playing a game or something."

Carlson realized over time that by asking clients to make a wild guess, he could challenge some of their resistance and reluctance to commit themselves. He began experimenting whenever a client said "I don't know" to have them just make something up: "I realize you don't have an answer, but if you did know, what form might that take?"

This is not unlike what solution-focused counselors do with the skeleton key, in which clients are helped to project themselves into the future to a time when they've resolved their problem. Once imagining that they have arrived at that state, they are then asked to look back into the past and report what they did to get there.

Whenever clients seem reluctant to commit themselves or provide a definitive answer, they can be invited to just pretend that they did know what to do. "Humor me," Carlson liked to say. "Just make something up. I won't know the difference anyway." Even if the answer was playful or bizarre, not altogether serious, it usually contained within it the seeds of their real yearnings and goals.

The objective of this and similar kinds of techniques is to override resistance to doing something unfamiliar, uncomfortable, novel, and completely different from whatever has been tried previously. Of course this is difficult and challenging, so it would be expected that there would be some pushback that might require a more circuitous route. There are so many strategies contained within the family counseling methods that essentially involve breaking existing patterns in order to discover alternative ways of interaction.

Some counselors find that counseling sometimes resembles a judo match. I don't mean that it is actually a competition between a client and counselor to see who defeats the other, but rather that the interactions, especially during the earliest stage, involve a series of cautious moves and countermoves. Clients often feel reluctant to commit themselves, so they stall and evade as much as they can get away with, avoiding accountability. When people say things like "I don't know," what they often really mean is "I'm not totally sure and I don't want to be wrong." But once the pressure is removed and they are invited to take a wild guess, they are often more inclined to say out loud what they are really thinking.

I mention this one fairly specific kind of response not as a panacea or foolproof strategy—although it does almost always work to prompt an answer—but rather as an example of the kinds of responses that experienced counselors develop and collect over time. Each of us has our own unique catalogue of favorite interventions that have been perfected over time and tested under fire. These are the standard, almost automatic ways we have learned over time to counteract resistance, sidestep excuses, and engage clients more directly in meaningful conversations.

Advanced Techniques That May Be Common But Are Very, Very Difficult to Do Well

Techniques almost never exist as an isolated entity, a mere tool that is applied to a given situation or problem. They are each embedded in a particular rationale, often part of a theoretical model from which it was spawned. Nevertheless, over time certain skills, interventions, and techniques have become part of generic practice, the kinds of things that any counselor might use regardless of his or her conceptual preferences. Interpretation is no longer exclusively within the purview of psychoanalytic practice any more than reflecting feelings is connected solely to a person-centered approach or role playing remains only a part of psychodrama.

One reason for the more general use of standard operating procedures is the greater acceptance that certain common variables are part of all good counseling. In addition, these integrative variables are actually the fuel that powers almost any technique. In summary, most techniques—and the theories from which they evolved—capitalize on the following factors, some of which we reviewed earlier:

1. Most approaches are designed to produce a kind of altered state of consciousness, a condition in which clients are more suggestible and most open to hearing things they may otherwise deny, avoid, or ignore altogether. It isn't just through formal hypnotic induction procedures that this occurs but in the simple, soothing voice we use to command attention and calm anxiety.

2. It is also fairly obvious that many techniques are designed to solidify and enhance the therapeutic relationship. Perhaps it is a bit of a stretch to call such efforts *techniques*, because instead they represent ways of being that strengthen the alliance.
3. Although cathartic processes were originally such an integral part of psychodynamic therapy, all of us now recognize that it is often useful to provide a forum for clients to talk about and work through their troubles and concerns, sharing aspects of themselves that may previously have been hidden or disguised. In any case, we often invite clients to reveal their deepest selves.
4. In different ways most approaches to counseling include some promotion of new insights, raising consciousness and awareness of some new and different facets of experience. Insight promotion techniques may focus on unconscious motives, underlying cognitive distortions, systemic influences, power hierarchies, gender scripts, culturally embedded norms, behavioral reinforcers, defense mechanisms, attachment disorders, and dozens of other things, but they all have in common an interest in increasing understanding of how and why problems develop in the first place.
5. If our goal is truly to promote lasting change, then we realize that promoting new insights, encouraging deeper awareness and understanding, delving into the past or repressed feelings, uncovering cognitive distortions, or discussing self-defeating behavior is often not nearly enough to make a difference over the long haul. That is why so many techniques have been designed to help clients rehearse new behaviors (role playing, enactments, etc.) and put them immediately into action as some form of systematic homework or personal application of ideas to daily life.

Personal Storytelling for Better or Worse

Located within the context of these relatively universal variables are a few skills/techniques that are indeed commonly used. But I consider them to be among the most advanced interventions, mostly because they are difficult to truly master. Take as an example self-disclosure, surely one of the most common techniques that counselors use—but also perhaps the one that is most often used inappropriately and introduced awkwardly. After all, any time we take the focus off the client and redirect it elsewhere, especially toward ourselves, we risk further invalidating and demeaning the client's already precarious self-image. We often end up elevating our own power in the relationship even further: "Look at me! Look how great I am and all the wonderful things I've done, and can do! Don't you wish you could be as great as I am?"

And yet I've found that there are times when our use of personal stories or disclosures can be among the most persuasive and powerful tools at our disposal. When well timed and carefully modulated, these stories or disclosures are known to reduce perceived distance with our clients.

They humanize us and provide opportunities for clients to more easily identify with us, seeing what we can demonstrate as far more accessible and within reach for them as well.

There are actually so many different techniques that counselors might use to share stories or disclose aspects of themselves in order to motivate or inspire their clients:

1. Sharing personal information to reduce psychological distance: "Yes, I have two children, both girls in elementary school."
2. Humanizing and personalizing themselves: "I am quite familiar with the concerns you describe. I also once struggled with feelings of isolation and loneliness until I'd had enough and decided to take action."
3. Teaching lessons: "I've found that sometimes it has been best for me not to force myself to do things that don't yet feel like they fit."
4. Demonstrating authenticity: "I feel really close to you right now, and it means a lot to me that you were willing to trust me with what you just shared."
5. Creating immediacy: "I'm aware that just as you said that, you seemed to pull away, to back off physically to protect yourself."

I mention the importance of immediacy as perhaps the one technique I find most challenging to pull off with sufficient deftness. It is one of the most powerful of all interventions because it brings the client into close contact with what is going on in the moment. Instead of talking *about* something, you are now focused on what is happening *right now.* There's no place to hide, and it's much more difficult to intellectualize and keep the issue at a distance.

Redefining the Problem

Although it is also a common technique with lots of different names, I find it especially difficult to redefine the problem well, that is, to sell a reconceptualization of the presenting problem in such a way that the client will take it in. It is usually the first step we take when a client describes what is bothersome, usually a variation of the themes (a) "It's not my fault," (b) "I can't help it," (c) "I've always been this way," or (d) "It's too big/complex/longstanding a problem to ever really change."

Clients bring to us issues framed in terms of intractable helplessness: "I'm shy, and I've always been that way" or "Everyone in my family has been depressed forever" or "I'm just addicted to failure. Everything I've ever tried has ended up a big mistake."

Of course all of these are distortions or exaggerations, so we use a variety of techniques to reframe, reconceptualize, or redefine the problem in such a way that it can be more easily addressed and resolved. Yes, just like the use of immediacy or self-disclosure, this is something we learned early on in our training, but I still find it among the most challenging strategies to do exceptionally well. Clients are often so vested in holding on to their previous self-definitions of the problem; they are often reluctant to surrender them to alternatives that imply that they have much greater responsibility and control than they might like to admit.

Masters Reveal Some Secrets

Michael Hoyt, mentioned earlier in the context of experimenting with alternative ways of engaging clients, has been known to switch roles with his clients in order to shake things up a bit. Hoyt learned this from one of his supervisors, who asked him to present a case even though Hoyt had yet to see a client he could introduce. "That's okay," his supervisor said. "How about if I present one to you and then you give *me* feedback?"

Looking back on this strange interaction, Hoyt concludes that this role reversal accomplished several goals. First, it demonstrated and modeled the proper way to present a case. Second, the supervisor could assess Hoyt's level of sophistication in terms of case conceptualization. Third, they could initiate a more collaborative relationship. And finally, he might even get some useful suggestions. As a result of this kind of more egalitarian partnership, Hoyt and his supervisor eventually became friends and coauthored articles.

Another example of a creative intervention is described by Michael Yapko, who once took an altogether different route than Carlson when a client responded to a critical question with "I don't know." In this case, when a woman reported that she felt "stuck" with a writing project, Yapko decided to explore how she prioritized what was important to her and how she decided what she gave the greatest preference. Her response was to become flushed and eventually stammer out "I, I, I don't know" reflecting her lack of reliable decision making strategy for the endeavor.

"That answer spoke volumes about what I would need to target in my intervention," Yapko explains. "She couldn't answer the question because she *didn't* decide what to do with her time. She wasn't proactive in deciding how best to budget her time. Rather, she was just reflexively responsive to the requests others made for her time." Yapko then realized that her generosity toward others was getting in the way of taking care of her own needs. Although this may seem rather obvious in retrospect, Yapko has been struck by how often other counselors in his place will instead try to find out why she wants to write in the first place or focus on her unconscious fear of failure.

Yapko's secret is to drill through some of these deeper, and perhaps irrelevant, issues and instead seek to depathologize behavior and identify specific skills that will better help clients meet their articulated goals. He believes that the "whys" may be interesting, especially to the counselor, but they don't necessarily fix the problem. "I don't need to understand *why* in order to understand *how.*"

Yapko's signature style is to first assess what the client has been doing to maintain the current situation and then collaborate to figure out how best to capitalize on existing resources and new behaviors that might be applied differently. "In our sessions, therefore, my client learned how to use specific situational criteria for determining when to say yes or no to a request rather than just following the reflex to say yes. She also learned how to tactfully and even charmingly decline invitations and manage others' disappointment. And she learned how to proactively mobilize her creative resources in new ways in order to fulfill her desire to write." Ultimately this led to her publishing seven books.

Yapko believes that *every* counselor has a few go-to moves that he or she doesn't really consider all that special or unique, and he is inclined to put this example in that category.

For those who balk at the idea that what they have discovered is all that unusual, his advice is to consider what you already do that seems effective and to keep a list of such things throughout your career. "You may be surprised how the list grows over time, not to mention the potential benefits of your list for other counselors and supervisees and, most importantly, for their clients."

Stephen Lankton, another counselor within the Ericksonian tradition, is known to use all kinds of rather inventive, mysterious, and seemingly crazy ideas to move his clients from their complacency. However, he cautions those who wish to imitate his style that such directives must be respectful of the client and used only during special and appropriate moments when perhaps usual methods are not useful. The goal is never for the counselor to appear to be brighter than the client or to outsmart him or her. "Truly the counselor ought to be kept in suspense and wonder as the client." Yet paradoxically—and remember that Lankton is big on paradox—as important as intuition and mystery are to his process, he also emphasizes that whatever we do or try should fall within our range of expertise and comfort. "This is not an intervention to be used when the therapist doesn't know what else to do." And yet—yes, here the paradox comes again—"Learn to be comfortable when you don't know."

Lankton specializes in the use of metaphorical allusions and ambiguous referents in order to access multiple modalities of internal processing. During previous conversations, he explained how his own experience and views were shaped by his encounters with Milton Erickson. Although hundreds of volumes have sought to decode the complex inner workings of the great master's hypnotic induction procedures, Lankton concluded that the best explanation is that Erickson often had no idea where his sometimes bizarre prescriptions to clients would lead. The key, according to Lankton, is that therapeutic tasks should be sufficiently ambiguous, but only slightly relevant, to the client's issues so that he or she is required to create or find meaning in the experience.

"Throughout my practice," Lankton explains, "I've noticed that some ideas spoken to clients rise to a remarkable level of importance and remain in their awareness for years, repeatedly helping them interpret options and solve problems. Those are the *ambiguous* ideas that are expressed with what appears to be a very high level of relevance to the listener." This insight comes from his own personal experience as well as his clinical practice.

Lankton's secret is thus incorporating the power of ambiguity as a tool to promote subtle forms of change. He points out that this stands in contrast to the usual cultural norms associated with precision and clarity but tends to work best when clients can perceive some degree of relevance to their own lives. Just as it isn't necessary for us to actually understand clients, so long as they feel understood, the goal is to promote conditions in which clients can recognize an appearance of relevance whether it is intended or not. This might actually be a good summary of the value of any technique, secret or otherwise: We must be able to help clients project their own experience into anything we do in such a way that they create meaningful value.

In the next chapter, we take up this subject in a different context, considering how techniques and interventions can often represent creative breakthroughs, not only in a given session but in terms of how we think about our work and lives.

CHAPTER 14

Creativity and Learning Far Afield

It was a tradition among the earliest theorists and practitioners in our field to learn about the intricacies of the human condition, as well as the nature of suffering and healing, from many different sources outside the realm of our discipline. Of course in those days, there was no body of knowledge and research in counseling from which to draw. Sigmund Freud discovered much of the inspiration for his ideas from the novels of Leo Tolstoy and Fyodor Dostoyevsky, the philosophical writings of Georg Hegel and Friedrich Nietzsche, and the paintings and sculptures of Michelangelo; he fancied himself as much an archaeologist, historian, and cultural critic as he did the founder of psychoanalysis. So many others have followed in his footsteps, delving far afield into any realm that might further enlighten their deeper understanding of people's experiences.

The Power of Direct Experience

Transformative travel experiences have had a powerful impact on the ways in which counselors develop as professionals and human beings. Freud spent as much of his discretionary time as possible on archeological digs, which he likened to the kind of excavations he was doing in his office. Other notable figures, like Carl Rogers, Albert Ellis, Alfred Adler, and Virginia Satir, constantly circumnavigated the globe in order to propagate their ideas. They were exposed to so many different cultures, languages, worldviews, and customs during their sojourns and workshop tours, and this helped them to broaden their thinking to be far more inclusive.

It is for this reason that I've often seen my role as a promoter of change within the context of being a travel agent of sorts. It seems to me that often what we do is help people to create novel experiences outside of sessions that are specifically designed to practice new behaviors. Although we can do that within clients' usual and customary settings, the potential for growth is significantly magnified in new and different environments.

For many years I've taken counseling students to work in far-flung places to practice their new skills, whether it's spending weekends in homeless shelters, weeks working with refugees abroad, or a month conducting home and school visits with at-risk children in Nepal. The challenges on these trips are so emotionally evocative and physically strenuous that it's almost impossible to return the same as when you left. People are required to meet their needs in ways they've never imagined. They are often flooded emotionally and way outside their comfort zones. They see and experience things they've never imagined. And they are provided with daily opportunities to process what they've witnessed, building deep relationships and developing new insights that will follow them for the rest of their lives. This makes what we might do in a classroom or traditional supervision feeble by comparison.

Based on those experiences, one of my secrets is that I've completely reconceptualized how learning takes place in such a way that the lessons stick over time. Unlike with passive learning in familiar and predictable environments, such as a comfortable office or classroom, I've found that the more novel the setting, the more likely it is that whatever happens will be remembered. I've since become a big fan of field trips, whether for clients or students. I've drawn inspiration from some of our field's historical figures who similarly experimented with alternative ways to get through to clients when talk alone wouldn't put a dent in their troubles.

For those of us who have been in the field for a while, it's sometimes hard to get much of a bang from consuming the same sources of learning over and over. Continuing education workshops may be mandated, but that doesn't mean we always learn very much from them: In many cases, participants just put in their time to get the credit for attendance. Likewise, although I've written so many books about counseling, change, and related topics, I sometimes don't learn much from these volumes in our discipline compared to the things I learn from more direct experience. After all these years, published ideas often seem reconstituted in a slightly different form. Journals might sit stacked on my dining room table for weeks before I browse through them for something that might be practically useful. However, I find that these days I learn so much more from reading great novels, biographies of interesting figures, social science literature presented in accessible ways as well as from dozens of daily publications, social media, and endless conversations when on the road.

Like me, Ashley is a counselor who has found that a big impetus to her growth and development was made possible not through more workshops and books on counseling but rather through delving into theater and acting to add to her skillset. I find it interesting and unique that Ashley specializes in theatrical therapy, a type of counseling that uses theater-acting techniques to help people overcome their fears. Her son is a prime example of how this works. He was born with Asperger's syndrome and has used theater therapy to overcome almost all the social dysfunctions that come with his syndrome. Ashley says he would become a character in a play and act in the manner of that character, intentionally playing someone who would perform and function socially the way he aspired to himself. Over a period of time, playing out these characters gave him confidence and the ability to learn how he should act appropriately in social settings. Right now he is a fully functioning adult living independently on the East Coast as a very accomplished musician.

Ashley's discovery was reinforced in other ways by practitioners who were interviewed by Amanda Johnson, a first-semester counseling student. "Every counselor I spoke to," she reports, "was involved in multiple and diversified facets of the profession, whether serving as board members, doing research, writing, or other things." Such creative pursuits seemed to immunize them against boredom or burnout by mixing up their daily routines. This pattern adopted by exceptionally creative counselors makes sense when you consider that so much of innovation arises from shaking things up, experimenting, pushing limits, putting ourselves in unfamiliar and uncomfortable situations. It is also one of the most crucial themes that we emphasize so frequently to our clients—how important it is get outside of our usual habits in order to test our limits and invent new ways of being that are far more effective and satisfying.

Accessing Alternative Modalities

Creativity holds a special place for Thelma Duffey, who was instrumental in founding the American Counseling Association division and journal devoted to innovative breakthroughs. She mentions one case in particular that stands out to her as an example of using different media like music to fortify the counseling process. Frida was one of Duffey's very first clients, although Frida was quite experienced, having consulted other counselors in the past for her longstanding pain, the result of childhood suffering. She had all but given up on the idea that she would ever recover; she believed that she had been a therapeutic failure and remained so. This represented a last chance for her to seek help, although she wasn't very optimistic that it would do much good.

"I learned quickly that this bright, kind, and passionate woman did not deserve the diagnosis she carried or the guilt that consumed her. From my perspective, she was stuck in grief, and part of our work involved helping her find compassion for herself. My hope was that she would grieve her losses and gain perspective. She had many gifts and talents, and she clearly wanted the freedom to enjoy these," Duffey says. This helped Duffey to focus initially on creating a sense of safety in their sessions as a first priority. And yet she also realized that a strong relational connection would only be a starting point, not nearly enough to break through Frida's self-defining failure identity. Somehow Frida had to break through her rigid mindset and entrenched defenses.

Duffey decided to let Frida take the lead as much as possible to access her creative spirit. "She'd bring in books and movies and her favorite music, which in many cases served as metaphors for her own feelings. By working with her creative resources, she eventually decreased her feelings of shame and was able to normalize a great deal of her experience. This helped her become open to new skills and opportunities and to seeing life in a more realistic way."

Frida had shared with Duffey that she had constantly felt judged by her previous counselors, that they had felt pity toward her. And yet empathy and relational engagement only set the stage for much deeper work. "I recalled a saying attributed to Hans Christian Anderson that when words fail, music speaks, and I've definitely found that to be the case. Knowing that Frida resonated with music, I asked if she was interested in creating a playlist, or musical scrapbook, of her experience. Quickly she was on board, and we used a musical chronology to represent her life journey. The point of this intervention was to help Frida connect with and tell her story, using music meaningful to her, and to help us set therapeutic goals. It was exciting to see Frida invest in this way."

The secret that Duffey developed into a robust creative technique began with Frida constructing and reflecting on a playlist of meaningful songs and then using them to process the significant events of her life. This was followed by using the music to reflect her current thoughts and feelings as well as those that represented her hopes for the future.

This is quite a good example of how a counselor combined her love of counseling with her other interests, one that hopefully resonates with certain clients who may feel blocked through traditional talk therapy. As Duffey says, "Many of us have had the experience of driving in the car, listening to the radio, and then we hear a song that completely takes us back in time. All of a sudden, we remember what we were doing, how we were feeling, and who we were with. With a click of a button, we're there. I believe this is what makes music a very powerful intervention tool."

Duffey is quick to point out that using creative vehicles such as music and other media does not generally follow a linear process. Sometimes a reliance on other modalities will trigger access to alternative modalities. "One day, as she was concluding our regular work, she brought in a handmade kaleidoscope as a gift. The kaleidoscope itself was amazing, but what I found most powerful—most meaningful—is that she described it as a symbol of our work together." Frida described to her counselor how "more and more I can modify some of my black-and-white thinking and create a world with more color and texture."

Just as Duffey accessed her creativity by embracing her inner spirit, so too has Jose Cervantes, a practitioner who has specialized in working with undocumented immigrants. His evolution as a counselor was transformed once he embraced the cultural heritage of his ancestors, especially that of his indigenous grandmother, who was a healer in her community. He began to incorporate some of the rituals into his practice using Native Mexican and Native American traditions.

"Robert was in the middle of a divorce," Cervantes explains, describing a case that captured his creative interests. Robert was a 51-year-old Latino who had been married for 25 years and served as an elected official in his community. He had been having a difficult time dealing with the losses that accompanied the breakup of his family. He also had a challenging history that included an unstable household growing up, bullying in high school because of his academic success, and betrayal by former colleagues. Needless to say, he had considerable trust issues, not the least of which was the result of the political arena he operated within.

It was primarily a spiritual journey with Cervantes that led to a deeper understanding of his issues and their meaning. "The emergence of a visionary experience served as a guide toward the latter part of this counseling process. Coupled with this dialogue came awareness for myself as a therapist in which I began receiving images, feeling states, and sensory reactions that complemented a fuller appreciation for the understanding this individual has undertaken and the affirmation of a higher consciousness that appeared to be influential in this therapeutic work."

Cervantes thus describes one of the frequent gifts that accompany creative work with clients—the reciprocal process of awareness and transformation that can take place among all parties involved. Quite a number of other exceptional counselors echo this point, recalling how their own most creative breakthroughs occurred as a result of feeling like they were truly partners with their clients during their journey.

Impediments to Creativity

One of the things that gets in the way of many counselors becoming more innovative in their work is the belief that creativity is always a huge breakthrough instead of a derivative, perhaps even modest, adaptation of existing knowledge or technique. So often when I have asked counselors whom I consider to be absolutely brilliant to describe their favorite method or strategy, they deny that they have developed anything original. This strikes me as much more than modesty, indeed it is a fairly limited conception of what it means to be truly creative. Almost no breakthroughs in science or art are created from pure imagination. Nothing is completely original; rather, it is a remix of what has preceded it. There are, however, several other blocks to creativity worth mentioning.

Certainty

As long as counselors believe that they know exactly what's going on with any client or situation, and enjoy perfect confidence that they are on the right track, there is no reason to experiment, adapt, or otherwise invent something new and different. I almost never feel absolutely certain about *anything,* so this isn't exactly a trap for me (I fall into other ones). There is probably no attitude that has led to more cognitive errors, moral lapses, and disasters than absolute certainty and the reluctance to consider alternative hypotheses in light of contradictory evidence. This is what often leads counselors to blame their clients for being resistant when things are not proceeding according to the usual plan instead of exploring other, perhaps novel, solutions to problems that have never been encountered before.

There are a few variations of this theme, such as insisting on total allegiance to a singular model because it is comfortable and familiar rather than borrowing ideas from competing paradigms that might offer additional therapeutic options. No matter how robust and comprehensive a particular theory, it can't possibly cover all possibilities, for all people, in all circumstances—an exception is perhaps laws of physics such as gravitational pull, but even that doesn't necessarily apply on other celestial bodies.

Another example of certainty getting in the way is sticking with tried and true favorite interventions and strategies because they almost always have proven useful in the past. It's the "almost always" that leads us to fail to recognize exceptions to the rule. For those counselors who work with especially difficult or challenging cases (And don't we all?), it's likely that other helpers who preceded us may have already exhausted the obvious therapeutic pathways, leaving us to construct something altogether new and different. If you are familiar with the biographies of some of our most prominent theorists, you will recognize the pattern of their being frustrated and stymied by existing dominant paradigms and so required to develop new ideas that were better and far more responsive to the needs of their clients. Because every theoretical structure was developed within a particular culture, era, and context, reflecting the values and preferences of its author, it is inconceivable that a model would work for each of us and each client without at least some refinement.

Putting Clients in Boxes

Earlier I discussed how diagnostic systems help us to organize and make sense of what we encounter, but they can also limit our ability and willingness to see each person as a unique individual. Once a diagnostic label floats to the surface of my mind, whether I try to bracket such thoughts or not, I start to feel more helpless and pessimistic about prognoses. A client tells me about a pattern of engaging in risk behavior, and I can't seem to block early training that sends out a warning to my brain: "Impulse disorder! Impulse disorder!" Or a client shares a story that sounds familiar to me, a likely scenario given how many hundreds of similar cases I may have treated, and I operate on autopilot, kicking into gear responses and strategies that seem obvious without questioning or critically examining whether they are truly the best options. I foreclose on the possibility of personalizing and customizing a far more creative strategy that could work wonders in ways I've never previously considered. For me, this is absolutely one of the most exciting parts of my job, the times when I feel like a collaborative artist more than merely a technician.

It is the perception of constraints, whether implicit in our preferred therapeutic model, diagnostic system, or agency policies, that limits creative enterprise. Once we tell ourselves that we aren't allowed to do something because it is against the rules, we surrender to convention. I'm not referring to ethical or legal rules either, those that are intended to safeguard client welfare, but rather those times when we fail to challenge the status quo just because things have always been a certain way. If this were the case, we'd still be treating people with bloodletting, leeches, lobotomies, and magic incantations.

Mistrusting our own intuition, informed by evidence, experience, and consultation, also limits creative options because we might feel that we are required to follow an established formula whether it seems to apply to the situation or not. It's back to all those voices inside our heads of previous instructors, mentors, supervisors, and writers who influenced us and initially showed us the way. But just as we tell our clients, overreliance on what others tell us creates indelible scripts that make it difficult to find our own path.

Secrets to Accessing Greater Creativity

We are all more than a little familiar with the research on what leads to creative behavior, whether in the context of scientific breakthroughs, artistic endeavors, or clinical practice. Throughout human history, innovations have arisen primarily as the result of questioning why things have always been done a certain way or challenging standard operating procedures because they don't seem to work very well in every situation.

Mutual Trust

In the context of counseling and other helping professions, creative actions usually take place when there is mutual trust in the relationship. Yes, it is important that clients trust us before much meaningful work can take place, but it is also helpful when we trust our clients to forgive mistakes and miscalculations when experiments don't pan out as expected. If we feel that we are constantly being critically judged, with each and every action examined under microscopic scrutiny, we are likely to be very, very cautious in what we do. Sometimes that is indeed the best policy, such as with particularly vulnerable or serious disturbed clients, for which a slipup can be potentially problematic, but most of the time we have far more latitude to try different things until we discover something that works best.

Admitting You're Lost

Until such time that you are aware that something isn't working, or that you really have little idea where things are going, much less where they've been, it's not likely that you will stop and reconsider the map you are following. Sometimes it's time to throw out the damn thing altogether and reconnoiter using your perceptual clues rather than relying on an obsolete template. Creativity often begins at the point at which you surrender to a position of not knowing and not understanding. After all, curiosity sparks innovation only after it is realized that existing knowledge or tools won't do the job.

- "I wonder why this client keeps putting herself in situations that inevitably lead to disappointment and frustration, even when she can easily predict the result?"
- "How come my client doesn't respond to the most gentle challenges, even when they are so carefully framed?"
- "Why is this interpretation not having any impact? It seems so obvious that this realization would explain the behavior."
- "It just doesn't make any sense that he claims his family supports him; it seems like they are actively blocking any progress. What the heck is going on?"

These are the kinds of reflective questions that lead us to throw up our hands in wonder, or perhaps frustration, but also to consider some unusual options that might not ordinarily be on the table.

Embracing Mystery and Confusion

Okay, this is a tough one. Most of us got into this profession in the first place because we so enjoy making sense of things, discovering the meaning and motives that underlie behavior, being able to explain phenomena that seem obtuse to others. I've mentioned earlier the work of Stephen Lankton and other Ericksonians who follow the tenets of many indigenous healers in which mysterious processes are embraced rather than explained. Try explaining what counseling is all about to any indigenous healer, as I've tried to do many times before; they find our profession ridiculous. "Wait a minute, you *talk* to people about their problems and you think that *helps* them? How do you even know what their problems *are? What?* They *tell* you?" That just makes no sense to them for all kinds of reasons. First of all, people don't really know what their problems are. Second, even if they think they do, they lie. Third, it's humiliating and shameful to talk about those things. And finally, does it really do much good compared to all the other therapeutic tasks that are part of their traditions?

When healers in other cultures do prescribe homework to their clients, it isn't the kind of logical activities that are clearly related to their problems and goals. As Lankton mentions, it is far better that homework be crafted in mysterious and ambiguous ways so that *clients* can create or find the meaning in the experience.

Brad Keeney is one practitioner who has sought to combine Western counseling ideas with ancient healing traditions from around the world. He believes that it is only by honoring mystery and embracing confusion that we can truly harness power and influence to promote change. He might very well ask a client to refrain from sharing a presenting problem out loud and instead think of a single word that captures the essence of what that difficulty means to him or her. Instructions might go something like this:

> Now I want you to take out a piece of paper and write down the word that holds for you the essence of your primary difficulty. Make sure the word

> you select is the best one among all those you've considered. Got it? Good. But don't tell me or show me what it is. Just write it down carefully. Use your best handwriting.
>
> Now fold the piece of paper carefully so it is perfectly aligned. Fold it again. And then one more time. Good. I know this isn't going to make a lot of sense to you right now, but I want you to trust me. Are you willing to do that? Because if you follow these instructions exactly, you are going to notice some incredible changes in your life, even some you haven't even anticipated. Ready?
>
> Okay, I want you to take off your left shoe. Yes, I'm serious. Please do that.
>
> Now place the folded piece of paper that contains that important word, the one that holds your problem within it, inside your shoe. Good. Now put your shoe back on your foot. Feels a little weird, doesn't it? But you can feel it there, can't you? Good.
>
> Now for the rest of the day I want you to walk around with the paper in your shoe and the word underneath your foot. Just become aware of that feeling. And then tonight, when you take off your shoe, the paper might be a little sweaty, but that's okay. I want you to place that paper that holds your problem underneath your pillow. And tonight you are going to have a dream . . .

And so it goes. These elaborate instructions might next include saving that piece of paper until the next full moon and then burying it underneath the branches of a favorite tree. And then . . .

Well, the point is that this therapeutic task is very much a trial or vision quest in the tradition of many native peoples. It is not designed to make sense or even be directly related to whatever the problem might be. Instead, it is designed to just shake things up, to get the person thinking, sorting out the mystery and confusion, and hopefully finding some relief in the experience.

It's not that I'm advocating that any of us try to pull off such a seemingly bizarre intervention. Truthfully, this isn't my style at all. I'm too inhibited to do this sort of thing. But I like the process contained within the example, that sometimes the things we do, or the things our clients might try, don't necessarily have to logically and rationally follow what preceded them. This might not be a first, second, or third therapeutic strategy; the times when we are forced to rely on creative strategies are only after we've exhausted everything else we know how to do.

Cognitive Flexibility

One definition of *creativity* is the ability to generate multiple solutions or options to a problem. This sort of fluency implies a level of suppleness that is often demonstrated in brainstorming activities when people are asked to list as many useful things they might do with a shoelace or a bobby pin as possible. They are encouraged to be not only practical but also downright silly. What this means, from a clinical perspective, is not getting locked in to just a few ways of doing this but being nimble enough to treat each client, every case, as a work of art different from anything we've done before.

Such flexibility is predicated on a willingness to challenge and question some of our most cherished assumptions regarding the way in which change takes place. It also means challenging conventional wisdom and so-called best practices. This is not to say that we should abandon them, as they are designed to follow available evidence and protect client interests; rather, we should continuously work to improve, update, and advance such guidelines to better reflect the vast diversity of our clients.

Counselors who specialize in working with refugee trauma, including refugees who have been tortured, raped, and abused, must adapt and structure their work in unusual ways. They can't expect their clients to show up in a clinical office because they are terrified of any symbol of government or authority, not to mention they have no reliable transportation. About three quarters of clients who do manage to schedule appointments never show up. So as a result, these counselors make house calls whenever possible and visit children in their schools, and the so-called counseling they use doesn't resemble anything close to what may seem familiar to most of us. They have to think differently about their work, about their place in their clients' lives, because *their clients* think so differently about their role and functions.

Courage

Let's face it: Creativity takes courage. Almost by definition, it involves an experiment, a testing of new boundaries, a leap into unfamiliar territory. The average amount of time it takes for a new innovation to become accepted by the majority is at least a decade or longer. It's not like you can announce some new breakthrough or creative advancement and others immediately offer their support and adoption. Initially such changes are experienced as threats; in some cases, others just don't get what the new idea or technology offers that is useful. The initial reactions to the iPod or iPhone exemplify the kinds of criticism of innovations that are beyond current levels of understanding. This is why Steve Jobs never viewed his products as designed to meet consumer needs or interests: He didn't believe that people knew what they really wanted until they were offered choices they never knew were possible.

Similar reactions were directed toward Carl Rogers when he first proposed his person-centered approach in an era dominated by behavior therapy. Other theoreticians were also treated brutally when they first introduced their novel ideas. Say what you will about Sigmund Freud, but the dude was relentlessly courageous to put up with all the criticism and abuse directed his way. And that was just for a year or two, but he came up with outrageous ideas (some since debunked) throughout his 60-year career. Even on his deathbed, after psychoanalysis had been recognized and widely disseminated, he was *still* fighting for new ideas.

The same holds true for any of us who sit in a classroom or staff meeting or group supervision session and share a variation of "I beg to differ." It takes guts and perseverance to stand up for one's beliefs when they oppose those of the majority. Hopefully, this is balanced with some significant, meaningful, and valid evidence other than just your opinion and felt sense.

Being Fully Present

Probably the most important secret of any creative enterprise is to be able to fully access as much data as possible, both from the external world as well as from one's own inner experience, perceptions, thoughts, and feelings. It is when we are most fully immersed in an experience that we are most likely to discover altogether new things about what is happening in the moment. It is this hyperawareness that often leads us to stumble on solutions to problems or novel responses that may never have occurred to us before. Whether this is called being *mindful* or entering a *flow state,* it is the ideal condition in which to access alternative ways of being in any enterprise.

Whether we are considering the conditions that are most likely to lead to creative innovation or simply greater immersion in each and every moment, it is by becoming more mindful that we enter those flow states that produce extraordinary satisfaction and insights. By its very nature, counseling is an exercise in being fully present, in which both (or all) parties concentrate and focus on what is happening within, without, and between everyone in the room. It is through such awareness that each of us learns to become more fully ourselves.

CHAPTER 15

Who Changes Whom?

If someone from another planet asked what it is that counselors actually do, we might describe our job as one directed toward promoting constructive changes in those who hire us. Our clients are troubled or dissatisfied in some way, and we collaborate with them to make adjustments in the ways they think, feel, and behave in order to function more effectively.

One of the secrets of our profession is related to how often we are the ones who are impacted, if not transformed, by some of our clients. This kind of reciprocal influence is both incidental and intentional. All the while we are doing our absolute best to persuade clients to do certain things and adopt certain attitudes, they are working hard to influence us as well. They want us to like them. Most of all, they want us to agree with them that they are not really the problem—it is everyone else who needs the help. In some instances, they are even trying to get inside our heads and hearts for reasons that go well beyond anything benign or merely curious.

Then there are the times we are merrily going about our business when—wham!—we are triggered by something a client mentions, perhaps an incident from our own past or a reminder of some issues we have yet to resolve. In other cases, the nature of our interaction with a particular person sets off some fireworks within our head or heart, something troubling or disturbing that penetrates us deeply.

Then there are the times we remain haunted in innumerable ways by the stories we hear during sessions. Clients tell us about their horrific abuse and neglect. They relate incidents in which they were subjected to unimaginable suffering. They relate their experiences with an emotional resonance that touches us in ways we couldn't have anticipated. We find ourselves thinking about them at the most inopportune moments.

We are also constantly moved by the courage and resilience that many people demonstrate, especially in the face of such challenging circumstances. We are brought to the brink of tears—or beyond—as a result of hearing about the ways that clients have managed to deal with circumstances that seem impossible. We hear stories of suffering from refugees or abuse survivors and wonder how anyone could possibly recover from something like that.

As mentioned in a previous chapter, we are also sometimes knocked off guard by the manipulation and deception that some clients bring into the room. Some people seem determined to get underneath our skin as a means of feeling their own sense of power. They lie to us, try to seduce us, and even deliberately betray us. I recall one couple I worked with over quite a long period of time. I not only got sucked into their problems but cared deeply about them. I imagined that once I fixed them maybe we could be friends someday.

Several months into the treatment, when we were making what I considered excellent progress, I heard the door open to the waiting room. I looked in to see the husband standing by a chair, signaling to me. "Yes?" I said automatically before retreating inside to wait for his wife so we could begin.

"Hey," he said in a whisper, looking back over his shoulder to make certain we were alone. "I just wanted to tell you that I'm having an affair. I've been with my girlfriend for over a year. But you can't tell my wife or it will ruin everything. This has to be confidential."

This was no time to have a conversation, so I closed the door and realized I'd just been ambushed. He must have been planning this for some time, as soon as he could get me alone. I realized that no matter what I did—keep his secret or disclose it to his wife—I was in an untenable position. We got through that session while I tried to figure out my next move, but by then it was too late. He disclosed to his wife that I knew his secret but had failed to share it with her. Understandably, she felt betrayed. But the real reason for all these games was that he hadn't paid for their sessions in many months, continuously promising me that he was waiting for an account to clear. Now he had the leverage he was looking for and so threatened to sue me for malpractice.

It wasn't just that I felt so betrayed by this client after having devoted so much time and energy to his case but also that I felt so incredibly stupid and played by him. Decades later I still feel the wounds. I still feel the hurt. Now the obvious question might be, what's all that *really* about? Why is it that the predictable, manipulative behavior of someone without much of a moral compass could not only fool me so completely but also make it so difficult for me to forgive myself? These are the kinds of interesting—and disturbing—questions that we are sometimes required to address as a result of relationships with some of our clients. We are, therefore, often changed in the process, for better or worse.

Some Questions to Consider

Allowing ourselves to be affected emotionally or personally by our clients or by what transpired during sessions was traditionally considered a no-no. It was evidence of a marked loss of objectivity, if not unresolved personal issues still in need of further work. It was called *countertransference* or *projective identification,* conditions that were viewed as compromising further progress. Counselors who admitted lingering feelings that were elicited during therapeutic work were in need of remedial supervision, perhaps even additional counseling. They were viewed as dangerous and certainly not safe for others to be around.

It turns out that some of the best secrets of our profession are the gifts we receive from our clients, the things they teach us about themselves, about the world, and even about ourselves. Every working hour we find ourselves engaged in the most intimate, interesting, stimulating, challenging, and at times disorienting conversations with people in the throes of crisis. Deep connections result from these relationships, some among the most intimate encounters we will ever experience. We talk about only emotionally evocative topics, taboo issues, and personal secrets that may have never been shared before. We do our best to enter into a client's world, not just the mind but also the heart and soul. We feel a degree of empathic engagement that almost allows us to hear and feel internal thoughts. So how could we *not* be affected and changed by these interactions?

Think back on all the people you have helped or tried to help in some capacity. Who stands out as the one client who had the *most* impact on you, personally and professionally? These changes you experienced could have been positive or negative but occurred as a result of your relationship with this person. The changes still endure to this moment.

What key dimensions of this relationship or helping encounter made it so memorable and influential in your life and work? How have you since processed what occurred and somehow integrated it into your life?

In the life of a counselor, almost every day there is a new lesson to be learned. Most sessions provide us with some interesting nuance under discussion that will continue to intrigue us long afterward. In many cases, we can't help but personalize some of the questions that clients regularly bring to us: What gives life its greatest meaning? Why do I keep engaging in behavior that isn't giving me what I want? What long-established patterns limit new options? Why do I remember certain things from my past but forget so many others? How is it that I ended up in my current situation? What new choices are open to me for the future? The list goes on and on.

We are constantly reflecting on the meaning of behavior, on the meaning of our *own* actions: "It's interesting that every time we get close to something, she abruptly changes the subject back to family. I think one reason that bothers me so much is that I sometimes do the same thing."

The reciprocal influence that takes place in counseling involves far more than such personal reflections. It is well known that one of the most significant operative ingredients of group counseling is the vicarious learning that takes place, how just by observing and listening to someone else work through a conflict or struggle it is entirely possible to engage in a parallel process and to do so privately and quietly without saying a word aloud. I've long found it fascinating after reading group member journals how sometimes the quietest, seemingly most disengaged people were actually those who really changed the most and initiated specific constructive actions.

If that phenomenon happens in therapeutic groups, why wouldn't it also become present in *any* such interaction between two or more people? All the while a client is talking we are of course focusing on remaining fully present, setting and enforcing boundaries so we don't engage in self-indulgent behavior or meet our own needs, and otherwise making sure that all we say and do is in the client's best interests. But there is also always present that whisper of an inner voice nagging in the back of our minds, making notes for later consideration:

- "Gee, why am I feeling so frustrated right now? What's *that* about?"
- "Yeah, that sure sounds familiar. I remember when I . . . Oops. Stay focused."
- "I can feel myself becoming a little uneasy as we get into that area. Is this about my client or is it more about me?"
- "That reminds me of something that I need to follow up with."
- "I feel like such a hypocrite that I haven't fully resolved that issue either."

These are just a few of the most obvious examples of the kinds of self-monitoring and growth that often occur directly, and often indirectly, as a result of work. Almost any professional would clearly recognize this and find the experience familiar. But the most secret part is that we don't often celebrate and honor this personal growth very explicitly. There isn't a counseling session, a supervision consultation, or for that matter a class we've ever taught that we aren't convinced afterward that we've learned something significant as a result. Sometimes it is just having a favorite idea challenged and thus expanded. We might discover a new adaptation or modification of an intervention or technique that can be applied in a novel, perhaps more effective way. We end up realizing that some aspect of our life is in need of upgrading as a result of some discussion. Sometimes the impact is more ethereal or spiritual in that we just feel this incredibly close, transcendent connection to another person.

There is nothing wrong with us! We are not weak or dangerous. We are alive and growing just like we want our clients to be. It is so important to relish and embrace these experiences when our clients help us gain new insights into ourselves. Counselors can profit if after each session or each day they ask the question "What did I learn from this experience about myself and my own life?" Without this type of intrapersonal reflection or self-reflection, we cannot continue the deep interpersonal work with our clients.

The gains for the counselor are nothing to be ashamed of. Extraordinary counselors understand that this is an important part of the process. We could not possibly have learned the things that our clients teach us. Learning to accept and embrace keeps us alive and able to effectively connect. We only worry that if others find out just how much we gain, they might want to charge us after each session.

The Stories We Hear

It's the stories we hear and hold that affect us most intensely, that continue to haunt us. Likewise, as already mentioned, it's the stories we offer to clients that they might find the most memorable aspects of our work together. And it's also interesting how sometimes the stories that clients remember are not necessarily the same as those we can recall.

Stephen Lankton sometimes runs into former clients who will ask him, "Do you remember that story you told me?" He might smile and nod his head, but truthfully the memory eludes him. "I did however recently cross the path of a former client of mine, Matt, from the time I lived in Florida. Quite by coincidence we were both attending an art fair in Ohio and looking at some photography when he recognized me. As might be expected, he briefly brought me up to date on his life since I knew him over 20 years ago." Lankton says that the ex-client ended the conversation by telling him how impactful a particular story had been that he had shared with him. Lankton remembers that incident all too well because of the client's remarkable response to it. In fact, it reminds him of a story.

"Matt came to see me because his wife wanted a divorce. She moved out from their home after his reaction to an automobile accident she suffered." After she had been almost blinded when shards of broken glass had embedded into her eyes, Matt's response was simply to tell her to get a job to take her mind off the discomfort. Needless to say, this was not taken well; actually it was the last straw for her, and she filed for divorce. That finally got Matt's attention and he consulted Lankton, hoping to get some advice on how to convince her to stay. Actually, that's not quite true: "It was far too late for that since she had immediately relocated out of state and moved in with another man."

In his initial assessment of Matt, Lankton found him both arrogant and a perfectionist. He was a professor of mathematics and engineering, obviously bright but convinced he was smarter than anyone else in the world, including his counselor. He admitted that he was really just seeing Lankton in order to show his wife he was willing to change for her—which he actually was not.

Lankton couldn't help but tell his client that quite honestly he didn't think counseling would help and that Matt wouldn't likely be able to hear anything that was said much less learn anything new. "He disagreed with me of course, and we went back and forth about this for some time. Finally, I explained the reason he would be a terrible client was because he would demand specific answers and prescriptions." After confronting this issue head on, Lankton also stated that even if Matt did agree to try anything new, he'd likely claim it didn't work, so any effort would prove futile and a waste of time for both of them. In order for counseling to be helpful, he further explained, Matt would have to do something that was beyond him at this point, to refrain from demanding specific answers.

Predictably, Matt argued about that as well and insisted that he was smart enough to do anything, including learn from ambiguity. Following the paradoxical strategy, Lankton eventually gave in and admitted he might be wrong, but only if Matt agreed to test this hypothesis. As you can readily see, there were many complex layers to what was going on, not only for Matt but also for his counselor. This encouraged Lankton to access his own creativity and prescribe a rather unusual homework assignment. "I told him to obtain a clear large drinking glass and fill it half full with colored marbles. Then he was to take that glass with him to every meal for the next week without fail." Before Matt could object, or even ask for an explanation, Lankton continued to instruct him that in the near future he was only to consume beverages—water, milk, tea, soft drinks, coffee—from this marble-filled glass.

Okay, I know what you are thinking, which probably parallels what Matt was considering: What the heck was *this* all about? But remember that Lankton's strategies are all about staying present with his clients, trusting his felt sense of what is going on, and then following a rather mysterious, ambiguous process that might lead to breaking older, entrenched behavioral patterns. He likes to keep his clients wondering. In this instance, he avoided all of Matt's questions and told him to simply keep track of his ideas about why he had been asked to do this seemingly nonsensical thing. After all, if he was so brilliant, surely he'd figure it out.

"The reader should know of course that I had absolutely no idea what he might gain from this activity; its intent was deliberately obtuse. All I knew is that what I was asking him to do was safe, ethical, and designed to get him thinking in different ways," Lankton says.

Not surprisingly, during their next session Matt reported that he was pretty annoyed with this whole thing but in order to prove his counselor wrong, and show him he could deal with ambiguity, he decided to stick with it. After just a few days he realized that he was becoming increasingly thirsty because it was so challenging to drink from a glass of marbles. This led to his insight that the purpose of the task must have been to demonstrate just how hard it is for anyone to get their needs met from him. "Although it appeared as if the marble-filled glass would quench his thirst, it really only delivered increasing frustration. No wonder his wife was so dissatisfied with him. Then he began to cry."

Lankton softened his voice and admitted that he must have been wrong and that indeed Matt could learn to deal with ambiguity even if his profession was based on precision and formulae. "In subsequent sessions Matt learned to embrace some of his tender feelings and inadequacies and was learning to accept the same in others. It was far too late to patch things up with his wife, but he soon met another woman and remarried. He eventually expanded his world in a multitude of ways, becoming a professional photographer and potter, and that's how I ended up meeting him again 14 years later at an art fair."

The interesting part of Lankton's story to me is not the remarkably innovative and wildly creative way he structured a successful intervention that was so far outside the bounds of the ways we might normally conceptualize a case but rather how the memory and impact of his relationship with Matt endured after so many years. It's not surprising that a client would recall so vividly such a bizarre from of counseling, but it is quite intriguing why we tend to remember certain clients over others. Among all the hundreds, perhaps thousands, of clients we might see in a lifetime, several touch us in ways that we will never forget.

Who Impacts Us and Why?

There are all kinds of possible reasons why some cases might stick whereas others fade from memory. Sometimes it is because the story we hear is so poignant, so moving, so powerful, that it becomes a living thing in our minds. Free associate for a moment about one such narrative you've heard from someone you helped, one that moved you to joy or despair. I once had a client who was himself a writer—and thus an incredible storyteller—who talked about the circumstances of his life with such vivid detail and incredible resonance that I found afterward that I thought the experience was mine. I've since learned about how mirror neurons in our brain make it possible for us to consume stories in films, shows, novels, or oral narratives, and we may come to believe that they are real-life experiences that we have endured—and in a sense they sometimes do feel just as real as anything we have lived. Surely you have had the experience in which you find yourself thinking, even worrying, about characters on a favorite show or series, as if these fictional characters are actually your friends. And in one sense, at least according to your brain, it really feels that way. We make strong emotional connections to people we read about or hear about just as we do people we know in person. And that helps explain why some client stories more than others feel so real to us long past the time when the sessions ended.

Counselors frequently point to cases they will always remember because they were so incredibly frustrating, upsetting, and challenging. Often they were failures, or instances in which we messed up in some way, although sometimes they could have also had reasonably satisfying endings. The brain is also programmed in such a way that we tend to remember such mistakes, hopefully so we don't repeat them.

Clients may also be remembered because the problems presented were so novel and bizarre. Memory retention is especially attentive to anything we face in our lives or environment that represents a novel problem or unusual situation that could possibly prove threatening if we are not adequately prepared to deal with it. Jon Carlson and I once collected stories from famous counselors and therapists about their most extraordinary cases, the ones that would instantly come to mind if they were asked the question "What's the most unusual case you ever treated?"

The idea for this project began when we considered some of the most bizarre clinical situations that we had ever faced. Carlson remembered immediately a family that he had been called on to help because it was discovered that after the husband had died, his wife had arranged to have the body mummified and perched on a chair at the dining room table. As if that weren't strange enough, the two children in the home were assessed and appeared to be relatively normally functioning. What impacted Carlson the most, however, wasn't just how weird this was but also how it pushed him to reconsider making absolute judgments about what would necessarily lead to emotional disorders and what might not. This led him on a different path in his thinking in a multitude of other ways, and he learned to withhold judgments and remain open to alterative worldviews that may not have been consistent with his own.

Carlson's most memorable case paralleled one of my own that occurred quite early in my life and career when I was somewhat sheltered and naïve. Given that I was interning in an psychiatric unit, it shouldn't have shocked me so much to encounter variations of behavior that were beyond anything I could imagine. In one of my first cases, a young man sought help for a putrid smell that resembled the odor of a cow. It turned out that this may have been a symptom of guilt after a longstanding sexual relationship with a member of the bovine persuasion. After an encounter like that, nothing much could shock me again.

There was a litany of similar stories from famous theorists we interviewed about the clients who not only changed them personally but also may have had a profound influence on the abandonment of previous ideas and the development of their seminal theories. Like with so many of us, their most impactful clients exerted their influence early in their careers when they were still formulating their ideas. Here are just a few examples:

- William Glasser, founder of choice theory and reality therapy, recalled a woman with an unusual eating disorder who insisted on snacking from alley garbage cans even though she was from an affluent family. He broke loose from conventions of talk therapy and decided it made more sense to take her outside for runs through alleys to practice restraint.
- In a similar vein, Arnold Lazarus, founder of multimodal therapy, was listening to a client complain about his fears of approaching prospective partners. So Lazarus decided to take the client out on a field trip to a local bar, not to learn successful methods to engage prospective women but rather to process feelings of rejection if they didn't respond to him.
- Susan Johnson, cofounder of emotionally focused therapy, recalled a memorable client who hanged herself in the basement just to time how long it would take her husband to rescue her.
- Jay Haley, one of the architects of strategic therapy, could never forget an 82-year-old woman he treated who was still working as an active prostitute to service young men who were attracted to a surrogate grandmother figure.

- Donald Meichenbaum, an important figure in both cognitive and constructivist therapies, was powerfully moved by a woman suffering from intractable grief after the death of her daughter. This case triggered some of his own worst fears as a father.
- Violet Oaklander, a well-known child specialist, had never forgotten a client she treated who refused to speak in sessions. Oaklander tried everything she could think of until she invited the young boy to bring in his pet lizard and snake. She then proceeded to pretend to counsel the reptiles as a way to communicate with the boy, who eventually responded only in the voices of his horned lizard or gopher snake.
- Brad Keeney, a former cybernetics theorist who found a new home within indigenous healing, had a breakthrough in his work when he helped a Native American medicine man who'd never had a vision. Keeney was able to access his own vision as the means by which to help the healer to find his spiritual path.
- David Scharff, a noted psychodynamic theorist, thought most about a family in which recovered memories played a huge role in their recovery. He believed that this single case taught him almost everything he'd ever need to know and understand about the therapeutic process.

The clients we tend to remember most clearly, and those who have impacted us the most, are usually the ones who tested our limits, led us into new territory, presented novel problems, introduced ideas we hadn't previously considered, and touched our hearts and souls. Although there has been so much attention on the negative, detrimental aspects of clients impacting us in the form of countertransference reactions, projective identification, compassion fatigue, vicarious trauma, manipulation, power games, resistance, and similar phenomena, the other side of the coin is that we receive so many incredible gifts from clients as a result of their trust, resilience, and courage. One of the most incredible aspects of being a counselor is that we have all these opportunities to live so many lives vicariously through our clients' stories. We learn so much about different cultures, experiences, and inner worlds. Even though it is not intentional, we grow and learn along with them. They teach us important lessons of life. They remind us of issues that we must tackle ourselves. Sure, they find our tender, vulnerable spots, but that is a gift as well in that it brings our attention to our own unfinished work.

Most of us have not been taught to embrace the changes and transformations we experience as a result of our work. There are many good reasons for this, because it is quite important that we maintain a certain control, avoid personal distractions, keep our personal stuff out of the room, and avoid indulging our own needs. But acknowledging that such efforts are absolutely critical, we can also recognize and honor afterward that counseling is, and always will be, a reciprocal relationship in which all participants present are moved and shaped by the encounter.

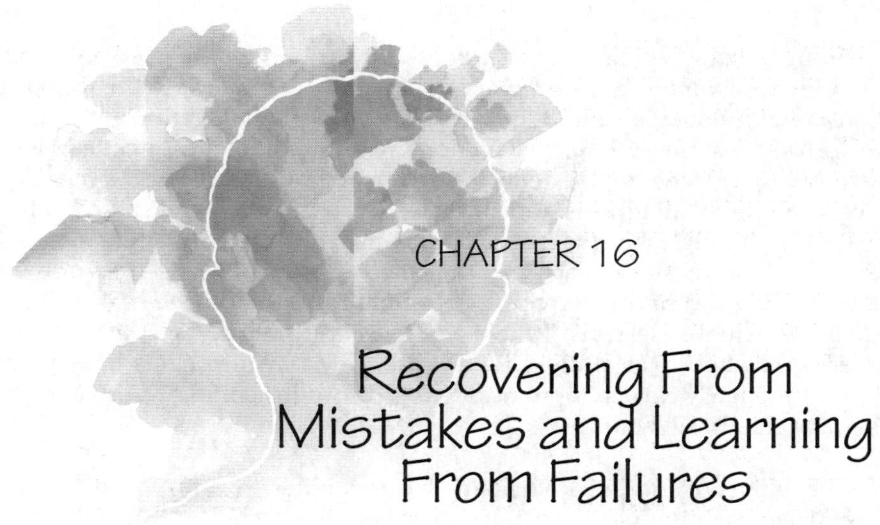

CHAPTER 16

Recovering From Mistakes and Learning From Failures

The scientific method is predicated on a process of making predictions, generating hypotheses based on limited observations. These projections are then tested with some sample that is believed to be representative of a larger population. The results, however, whether they confirm or refute what was prophesied, hopefully lead to generalizations that inform clinical practice. But there are always exceptions, anomalies, outliers that are located way outside the normal curve. These are the clients who don't fit our diagnostic categories very clearly or those who don't respond to normal protocols. They are often annoying and frustrating cases because they lie outside our realm of experience. They often lead to mistakes, misjudgments, and failures.

And yet it is precisely these exceptions to the rules that offer us the most interesting knowledge, that make our theories more robust and responsive, and that lead to breakthroughs. They are indelible lessons that we are more inclined to remember than any success or triumph. And it is also the outliers, the strange and unusual cases, when something goes wrong or doesn't follow the predicted path, that lead to most advancements in knowledge and science. One reason it's so important to acknowledge when we don't know or understand something is that we can recover from a miscalculation and change directions in a more productive strategy.

Failures That Are Never to Be Forgotten

Perhaps *recovering* isn't actually the most appropriate word to use when processing and learning from mistakes. Whether we are talking about the practice of counseling, medicine, or any other profession, failure usually occurs not because we lack knowledge but rather because we fall into skewed or limited thinking about what is going on. We become overly attached to a diagnostic impression or conceptual framework that prevents us from actually seeing more clearly other possibilities. We latch onto an idea or viewpoint and then remain reluctant to abandon it in the face of contradictory data, scrambling for reasons to explain the anomaly.

In his book *How Doctors Think*, Jerome Groopman cites a colleague, a cardiologist, who kept a detailed log throughout his 30-year career of every single misdiagnosis and mistake he ever made even though his colleagues thought he was crazy for doing so. It turns out that increased expertise and mastery is actually the result of such honest self-scrutiny. Rather than hiding or denying our failures, we should be embracing them as valuable lessons. I have written about before (and intend to keep remembering as often as I can) one of my favorite clients who was presenting fairly clear symptoms of panic disorder. I could confirm every item on the list of symptoms:

- Feelings of sudden, unexplained, unrelenting anxiety
- Heart palpitations, sweating, shortness of breath
- Trembling and shaking
- Nausea, dizziness, and faintness
- Fear of losing control
- Belief that he was dying

Because heart, lung, and thyroid problems had already been ruled out by his referring physician, it was pretty obvious what was going on. That helped me to focus my initial diagnostic questions on a history of anxiety and panic disorder in his family. (His mother had also had similar problems—or at least it seemed so.)

Over the course of several months, we connected in a remarkably intimate relationship. He was one of my absolute favorite clients because of his willingness to go deep as well as his complete openness and honesty. We were about the same age, and I found myself thinking that I wished we could become friends because I liked and respected him so much. We explored his past childhood issues, talked a lot about frustrations with a stalled career, and investigated an assortment of possible causes that might be triggering the attacks of anxiety. And yet . . . and yet . . . the symptoms still continued unabated in spite of my most insightful observations and deft interventions.

I interpreted the resistance as evidence that he wasn't yet ready to let go of the symptoms because of likely secondary gains. He thought that was an especially intriguing idea, so we spent many subsequent sessions exploring how these symptoms might be serving him in some way, perhaps as an excuse for not taking more direct, proactive action in his life. He also had a ready excuse for not doing things or going places that he wished to avoid—after all, the panic attacks might strike at any moment. We agreed that the symptoms might also be a way for him to feel a closer affinity to his mother, from whom he felt estranged. And we also shared the belief that the symptoms were designed to get his attention to address some previously unresolved issues.

Even though we both enjoyed our intense and fruitful conversations over a period of months, we finally reached a consensus that because the symptoms had not diminished in the least, perhaps it was time to take a break for him to do some of the reflective work we had previously discussed. He was so incredibly grateful for our time together and apologized that he couldn't have been a more cooperative client; he felt bad that he had somehow let me down because he hadn't been cured.

As the months continued, I thought about him often, wondering how he was doing, and so I was delighted when he called for an appointment almost a year later. When he walked into the office, we gave each other a warm hug.

"So," I began, "it's great to see you again, and I'm so glad we can now resume our work together."

He looked immediately uncomfortable, finally saying in a hesitant voice, "Well, actually I'm not here to continue sessions exactly."

"No?" I answered, somewhat surprised.

"I just wanted to give you a report on what happened after I left."

"Sure, sure," I encouraged him.

And then what ensued not only knocked me for a loop but forever altered the ways I think about what I do and how I do it. The client explained that soon after our sessions ended, he decided it was time to literally move on in his life, so he put his house up for sale. During the inspection prior to closing, he was required to have someone come in to check the functioning of the appliances. It was discovered that his furnace had been malfunctioning for quite some time, leaking carbon monoxide throughout his home. "Haven't you noticed feeling sick, dizzy, and nauseous?" the inspector asked.

So all this time he never needed a counselor, just a furnace repairman!

This is the sort of spectacular failure that none of us could ever forget. It tempered my arrogance, my delusional certainty about what I think is happening with any client, much less myself.

What *Is* Bad Counseling Anyway?

Failures do not necessarily imply that the counselor conducted lousy clinical work; after all, the client is at least 50% responsible for the ultimate outcome. There are times when we might actually perform rather brilliantly and it still doesn't make much of a difference. And then there are times when the eventual result is not so much the fault of the counselor or the client but rather influences that are beyond anyone's control—family meddling or other external factors. Nevertheless, I've been fascinated by the ways in which some counselors keep any negative outcome at a distance by providing ready excuses or refusing to acknowledge mistakes. In a previous project, Jon Carlson and I interviewed famous therapists as we had done for other projects that I've mentioned, but this time we picked a tough one, asking them to share the story of their worst failure, their most egregious mistake. Not surprisingly, there was considerable reluctance to do so, especially among prominent individuals who make their living by promoting a methodology that is often marketed as being almost foolproof. One of the facets of these conversations that I found most interesting was related to how these exceptional counselors defined failure in so many varied ways.

I especially liked the way in which Arnold Lazarus and Violet Oaklander readily accepted responsibility for those times. Michele Weiner-Davis labeled *failure* as not so much making a mistake but rather making the *same* mistake over and over. She provided a pretty amusing example of this when she recalled how she had been supervising a counselor behind a one-way mirror. If she ever had an idea or a suggestion for the counselor in the room, she would call in to provide the advice, a method that seems quite intrusive but certainly effective in providing needed support. Once Weiner-Davis called into the session when she had a brilliant plan to put into motion. Before the counselor could finish a few sentences, the client held up her hand.

"Wait a minute," she said. "Is that Wiener-Davis lady behind that mirror?"

The counselor was stunned for a moment but finally nodded.

"Well, you can tell her for me that I was in here a year ago and she tried that shit with me then and didn't work. And it sure as shit isn't going to work now either."

Following a similar theme, John Norcross, Peggy Papp, and Dick Stuart, each representing very different theoretical orientations, all agreed that their conception of failure was defined not by making mistakes so much as being consistently inflexible and reluctant to make needed adjustments. This was also echoed by Art Freeman, William Glasser, and Arnold Lazarus, who felt that bad counseling most often results from arrogance, overconfidence, and the counselor's own narcissism.

Quite a different perspective was described by myself, Sam Gladding, and Michael Hoyt, who thought of lousy counseling as more of an internal feeling of ineptitude when we feel lost and have no idea where things are going. However, Frank Pittman and Francine Shapiro explained this a bit differently in terms of making invalid assumptions that might lead us stubbornly astray. Others, such as Steve Lankton and Scott Miller, believed that ultimately the assessment is determined purely on the basis of whether the client becomes better or worse as a result of the sessions.

A compromise and summary position might best explain the primary causes of failure and ineffective counseling as the result of four different but interconnected variables.

Client Variables

Clearly the single most important predictor of success or failure in counseling is related to what the client brings to the encounter. If motivation is low, expectations are unrealistic, and hidden agendas are operating behind the scene, the prognosis is poor. In addition, if the client has a limited capacity for insight; a florid personality disorder; or a controlling, manipulative interpersonal style, that also doesn't bode well for the outcome. Some clients are inclined to sabotage treatment because of secondary gains they enjoy as a result of remaining stuck: On some level they are committed to a level of inertia in order to avoid taking risks or venturing outside the comfort zones.

Michael, for example, worries incessantly about everything—the weather, the economy, traffic, his health and finances, but mostly what other people think of him (which is that he is annoying because he worries so much). In response to each and every strategy introduced in counseling, whether mindfulness based or cognitively oriented, and even a trial of antianxiety medications, he reports complete failure to alleviate his symptoms. But it turns out that his behavior pattern actually gives him an excuse to avoid doing anything that he'd rather avoid. If he doesn't want to go somewhere or do something, he can just complain that he can't pull himself together. "It's not my fault," he whines. "I just can't help it. You *know* how difficult this is for me."

Counselor Variables

If clients often bring untenable expectations into counseling, so too do counselors entertain goals that are beyond what is reasonable. Sometimes we may lapse into savior mode in which we inflate our sense of power, truly believing that we have the power to cure people regardless of their own willingness and ability to change according to our preferences and pace.

Counselors' negative attitudes and rigidity also sabotage potential progress, as I discussed earlier when I mentioned the reluctance to abandon favored strategies even when it is apparent that they are neither appropriate nor effective. It is arrogance as much as any other characteristic that might lead us to miss cues and persist in directions that are less than optimal. It also doesn't help when counselors misperceive or misdiagnose client issues, bungle clinical skills, cross inappropriate boundaries, or engage in actions that are clearly counterproductive.

Finally, our own projections, distortions, and countertransference issues may get in the way. I've often felt provoked by clients who serve in authority positions and appear to do so in heavy-handed, autocratic ways. For example, I know I was less than accommodating with one client who very much reminded me of my school principal, who had given me a hard time.

Extraneous Variables

Many influences outside of our control affect the ultimate outcome of counseling and can lead to failures no matter how skilled we might be or even how cooperative and determined the client feels. Most obviously when fees are involved, things can end rather quickly if insurance or third-party payers cut off support or a job or income is lost. When there is an enmeshed or particularly dysfunctional family structure, one that is organized around codependency, any progress made in sessions can easily be undone. Likewise, if the client has no stable support system at all among family and friends, it can be difficult for counseling to ultimately succeed.

And then there are those instances in which a peer group actively seeks to undermine what goes on during sessions. "Are you still seeing that stupid counselor?" a friend asks while sitting in a bar over drinks. The client is sipping a club soda over ice to keep his friends company, as he has struggled with addictions to alcohol and prescription drugs for many years.

The client just nods and looks around the bar, hoping to change the subject. But it is not to be.

"Yeah," another friend chimes in. "I heard that counselors just brainwash you into thinking you are some helpless idiot. What you really need is a good stiff drink to help you settle down. Here, have a sip of mine. One little taste won't hurt you."

Of course when one person in a peer group makes a dramatic change in behavior, especially related to indulgences that others persist in even though it is destructive to them as well, it is often experienced as destabilizing and threatening. We see this phenomenon constantly whenever clients decide to change some longstanding pattern that requires others in their world to adapt or else to come to terms with their own dysfunctional behavior.

Process Variables

Whereas the previous factors relate directly to characteristics and behaviors of individual participants, there is also sometimes an interactive effect in which both client and counselor are triggered by each other. Sometimes personalities and interpersonal styles are incompatible. Sometimes cultural differences between the participants are so vast that they just don't speak the same language, which results in frequent misunderstandings. There was a time I was working in Iceland with a client whose presenting issue was a lack of intimacy in her life. She complained that she had had a series of brief, sexual encounters with partners but rarely if ever any kind of enduring relationship. Actually she described how every Friday and Saturday night she would head to the bars and clubs, hook up with a partner for the night, and then never see the guy again.

Although I tried to be as culturally understanding and responsive as I could, given that her behavior was somewhat normative for young people in Reykjavik at the time, the differences in our age, language, and relationship expectations were so vast that she constantly felt judged by me (which she was). In turn, I would overcompensate and try to be as solicitous as possible, which she found even more disingenuous and offensive. We spent a lot of time arguing with each other and never made much progress, both of us pretty frustrated. This case exemplifies many of the process factors that are influenced and affected by both an inadequate therapeutic alliance as well as cultural misunderstandings.

Leah Brew, a specialist in cultural misunderstandings as they play out in counseling, believes that so many problems come down to us as practitioners not being fully aware of how our own cultural scripts, values, and traditions affect what we do and how we do it. Brew believes that we can never fully grasp and understand all the nuances that have a role, and it is so important to invite client feedback so that we can closely monitor our lapses and mistakes. She cites a recent example of this when she was supervising beginning students who were practicing basic skills. One student, who served in a leadership role in her church, had been discussing some tough decisions she had to make. "In an attempt to help her perceive the consequences of her decisions, I had asked if her superiors were conservative and more judgmental in their religiosity. The student agreed that this was likely true and then changed the subject."

After the session was over, the student asked to meet with Brew, clearly anxious and uncomfortable. After dancing around for a bit, she finally disclosed that she felt offended and judged by what she sensed was her supervisor's critical values about what it meant to be a conservative Christian. Brew immediately apologized rather than explaining her intention or defending herself. "The student talked about her fear of being in a program where her religious culture may not be honored. I validated that she may be right and that she may hear derogatory statements from others. We talked about in which contexts she would want to confront the offense and which she would let them go." The conversation ended with Brew inviting her to meet with her any time in the future when she felt her own views weren't being heard and respected, as this was likely to occur.

"So this is my secret: I have to be explicit about asking for feedback and do so in a way that seems open and accepting. I know that I will never be completely culturally sensitive, but I aspire to become more so as much as I can. I know that no matter how hard I try I will make comments that can sometimes wound others. So I have to validate the experience of the other person, own my offenses, and sincerely apologize for them. This is how I maintain strong relationships with students and clients."

What Brew considers unique about her approach is not simply that she strives for greater cultural sensitivity, which is a foundation of our profession, but rather that she accepts and readily acknowledges her own lapses. Once she can recognize them, she is then in a position to correct any misunderstandings and learn from those experiences.

Processing Mistakes and Failures

It is a familiar refrain from anyone, in any profession, who has been extraordinarily successful that life's greatest lessons come from efforts that didn't work out as anticipated. Thomas Edison, for example, didn't admit that he ever failed at anything, just that he found thousands of ways his efforts didn't work. I recall an interview with Arnold Lazarus in which he explained, similarly, that he really didn't think in terms of ultimate success and failure but rather smaller, incremental goals that could be more easily achieved. Although South African, he used an American football metaphor: He didn't see his job as helping clients score touchdowns but rather as helping them get a little further downfield, perhaps to reach a first down.

It is often useful to ask a few important questions when processing unsatisfactory outcomes, whether in counseling or in other aspects of daily life:

- *What are the signs that counseling isn't working?* Until such time that we recognize—and acknowledge—that what we are already doing is ineffective, there isn't much chance that we will try something else that could be more helpful. This sounds rather obvious, but people can be stubbornly resistant to surrendering familiar strategies, even when they clearly prove useless.
- *What secondary gain is the client celebrating as a result of the failure?* I find it immeasurably helpful (and one of my favorite secrets) to constantly ask myself what clients (or anyone else) get out of remaining stuck. It is usually some variation of the themes that they (a) get attention and pity from others, (b) have an excuse for avoiding the hard work and effort involved in change, (c) can blame others or external factors for not getting what they say they want, (d) have a means by which to manipulate or control others, and (e) can maintain a sense of perceived self-control by messing this up on their own terms.
- *Has the problem been defined in such a way that it cannot be resolved?* Reframing is hardly a secret, but we sometimes may forget that failure is indeed as much a state of mind as it is a condition of circumstances. Or to put it another way, in the words of a song by Crosby, Stills & Nash from long ago, "If you can't be with the one you love, then love the one you're with." This isn't an admonishment to settle for less than anyone deserves but rather a reminder that sometimes stated goals are initially out of reach—at least until such time as new skills are learned. When clients describe themselves as "losers," "shy," or similar self-identifiers, our job is to help them to reconceptualize those labels, such as "Sometimes I behave shyly."
- *How have I been attempting to disown responsibility for what is going on?* This question relates to an earlier point: When clients appear difficult, we may tend to blame them for being resistant or uncooperative, as if it were solely their fault that things aren't going well. Although it is true that some clients can be incredibly challenging, and that almost anyone would agree that they are obstructive, it still doesn't change the fact that *every* problematic relationship is an interactive phenomenon. Even if our contribution to the impasse is only 20%, or however that might be measured, that still provides a bit of leverage for us to honestly consider how we might be making things worse than they need to be.
- *What interventions have been most and least helpful?* It helps to take a detailed and systematic inventory of exactly what is failing and in what circumstances and conditions. Although supervision or even peer consultation helps a lot with this process, there are still a number of self-supervision steps that can be followed. In a sense, these

very questions are specifically designed to facilitate such a critical assessment of what is going well, what has not been useful, and what alternative strategies might be used to change directions.

Just as in solution-focused and problem-solving counseling, the intention is not so much to discover the perfect answer on the first or even second try but rather to cease doing things that are virtually guaranteed not to work because they've been attempted a few times already. Only after we stop clearly ineffective actions do we open up possibilities for discovering other options that may prove more useful. Once again, if the alliance with the client has been solidified, we are afforded many opportunities to eventually find the best combination of alternatives.

- *What was the turning point when things started slipping downward?* It's important to be able to identify when counseling stopped being helpful (unless it began on the wrong foot in the first place). Was there a particular trigger or critical incident that appeared to change things?

  I often rely way too much on humor in my work, whether in counseling or in teaching. As I've aged, I've become even more irreverent, spontaneous, even impulsive in my actions. I'm more inclined to use colorful language. I sometimes insert stories or examples that less enlightened or more sensitive people might conceivably find off-putting. Even though I know that sometimes it's risky for me to tease someone, or to vigorously challenge something that I find utterly ridiculous, if I watch closely enough I can tell immediately when I've gone too far. I strongly agree with Brew's recommendation mentioned earlier that when we are aware that a client appears offended or taken aback in some way, it's so important to apologize and do damage control. In fact, I'd say that one of my most valuable secrets is to be fearless when admitting I am wrong, or at least inappropriate.
- *What have I been expecting that is unrealistic or beyond the person's ability?* One of the major causes of client resistance is when we ask (or even require) people to do things they are neither ready nor able to do. My own impatience gets in the way in this regard. It often feels like I know *exactly* what a client should do to make things better: Start exercising. Lose weight. Stop drinking so much. Go back to school. Find another job. Dump that loser partner of yours who is making you miserable. Stand up for yourself. But so often these prescriptions (or admonishments) are hardly appreciated, much less acted on. If only counseling was as easy as

  Client: I drink too much.
  Counselor: Okay then, stop drinking.

or

  Client: I keep getting in trouble at school because I talk back to my teachers.
  Counselor: If I were you, I wouldn't do that anymore.

- *Who has an interest in sabotaging the treatment?* This refers back to the external factors outside of our control that can nullify anything that occurs within sessions. Most often these include family members, friends, colleagues, or toxic acquaintances who are threatened by the changes a client is making and so launch a counterinsurgency campaign. That's why it's important to help immunize clients against anticipated threats or challenges, what motivational interviewing refers to as *relapse inoculation*.
- *How have I been negligent?* Okay, here it is. The naked truth. Put aside all the excuses and reasons for the poor progress. Stop focusing on the client's role in the difficulties. Let go of any limitations of your theory or problems with technique. Stop seeking support from colleagues to justify your actions. You don't have to put this so bluntly in the progress notes or in a narrative to your supervisor, but true confession—what did you mess up? In order to learn from mistakes, it's first necessary to admit they occurred. It is so, so frightening and requires a tremendous amount of courage to acknowledge errors in judgment or execution. That's how you get sued or even fired. Nevertheless, at least admit to yourself what you didn't know or understand or where you failed miserably. You don't have to broadcast it to the world, but pay close attention so you don't make the same mistakes again.

Each of these questions invites you to look closely at who you are and how you characteristically operate. They help you to answer the most important question of all: What can I learn from this experience to help me grow?

That is the precious gift we receive from our mistakes and failures. That is what teaches us most memorably to stretch beyond what we think we know and understand.

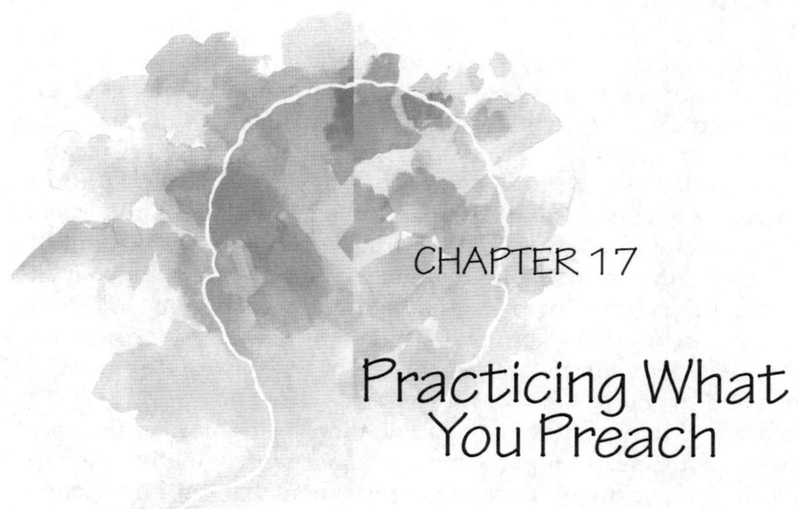

CHAPTER 17

Practicing What You Preach

A colleague of mine was traveling to Mexico on a family vacation and, upon arrival, discovered that the airline had lost all their luggage. They were there for a week without a single item of their personal clothing or things. They had to restock anything they might need, purchase supplies, and survive with the most basic necessities they could find.

"So that must have been awfully frustrating."

He shrugged. "Hey, what can you do?"

"You mean you weren't upset that the airline lost all your bags, everything, even your toiletries, your children's toys, camera, everything?"

"How was becoming angry going to help anything?" he answered with a smile. "The bags were gone, but that didn't mean we still couldn't treat it as a grand adventure."

However impressive this response might have been—taking things in stride, telling oneself (and others) that there's nothing that can be done, making the best of an annoying situation—it is actually the perfectly logical reaction of most any counselor who helps people with these sorts of disappointments for a living. After all, what we do is teach clients to talk to themselves differently about the inevitable frustrations of life.

If there is one thing that our profession teaches us, even if it is rarely explicitly mentioned, it is that everything we learn in the realm of therapeutic skills and techniques most often works just as well on ourselves. When we challenge a client's dysfunctional beliefs, we can't help but ask ourselves the extent to which we might hold similar attitudes. When we tell a client it might be advantageous to stop doing something that is clearly not producing a desired outcome, we sometimes consider the ways we might be stuck in the same self-defeating cycle. When we urge others to maintain healthy lifestyle patterns with regard to eating, sleeping, and exercise, it's hard not to apply such advice to our own lives. Every single day we talk to people about ways they can become more fully functioning in their lives, and it's hard not to take such advice personally.

It might be delusional to reject our own counsel, but it's not as if this doesn't happen quite often. There are *way* too many members of our profession who can't—or won't—apply to themselves what they teach and advocate for others. They pressure their clients to take constructive risks and experiment with unusual ways of approaching their difficulties but may be reluctant to do anything but stick with the familiar and comfortable in their own lives. They may preach passionately about the power of deep intimacy and solid relational connections but fail to make it much of a priority for themselves. They talk a good game when the meter is running but don't apply what they know, understand, and can do in the arena where it matters most. In other words, some among us are frauds and hypocrites.

There are few things more bothersome then seeing or hearing about colleagues who are mean spirited, vindictive, petty, manipulative, perhaps even toxic in their behavior. They might tell others that it is important to live with integrity, honor, and compassion but fail to do so during their daily interactions. They are instead self-important and self-serving.

Without belaboring this disappointing phenomenon of counselor incongruence, inauthenticity, and at times personal dysfunction, let me just say it would be a wonderful world indeed if counselors could truly do what they ask of others. Of course we are all works in progress. Each of us is doing our level best to keep things together. We become triggered by things that are brought up in session. We remain haunted by unresolved issues in the past, some of which are played out as a parallel process during sessions. As a result of our deep conversations with clients about their most vulnerable areas, we can't help but confront some of our own. The important question related to this collateral damage, which is really offered up by the universe as a gift to get our attention, is what we choose to do to put our own best advice into action. To what extent do any of us actually practice what we preach?

Our Authentic Selves in Action

Miguel Gallardo, introduced earlier, believes that one of the reasons he is effective in his work is because he quite literally has "face validity." Initially people might come to see him because of his Latino surname and his fluency in Spanish, but that only takes him so far. "Ultimately I have a responsibility to create a therapeutic relationship that is congruent and in alignment with the world in which they exist." He takes issue with many agencies and practitioners, even within the Latino/a community, that nevertheless follow policies and procedures that are narrowly measured by standards that really don't apply to this population. "I don't blame them; they are just trying to survive within systems that really don't care about people. These systems may start off caring about people, but most end up succumbing and perpetuating the exact oppressive practices they are working against."

Gallardo admits that he works from a privileged perspective because the counseling he does is pro bono, which allows him to make choices that are not possible for those who must earn income within the system. He is also able to rely on strategies that he sees are not only congruent and authentic but also well suited to his client population. "I see self-disclosure as a therapeutic technique and not an ethical dilemma to be avoided. I ask my clients during the first session if there is anything that they want to know about me before we begin our work together." Although this invitation is rarely ever accepted by clients, he feels it is important to demonstrate this kind of transparency.

Gallardo remembers a 69-year-old Mexican man who was referred to him after an accident at work that left him physically disabled and emotionally vulnerable. Their conversations together were not just about presenting symptoms but also about entrenched racism, systemic oppression, and feelings of being disenfranchised. This is the lived experience of those who have felt they've not been heard and understood. "I need to be able to have these conversations with my clients and to disclose my own experiences with racism and oppression and, more importantly, to validate *their* experiences as based in reality."

Gallardo wonders why when a client presents with depression, or anxiety, or some other symptoms, we immediately look them up to decide what to do and which technique or empirically validated strategy to use, "but when it comes to working with those living in poverty, dealing with oppression and racism, and who live from day to day, we become paralyzed and attempt to fit their 'problem(s)' within our own comfortable cognitive schema that makes us feel more competent in our work with them. This isn't about individuals but the systems in which we are embedded that continue to misguide us as a way to maintain our already existing power structures that continue to privilege the worried well."

When Gallardo speaks of using his authentic self, or rather *being* his authentic self, he often finds himself in a role very different from the one for which he was originally trained. "This includes my willingness to address issues such as power, privilege, racism, including my own experiences in all of these areas. It means not just talking about what is 'wrong' with a client but also understanding felt experiences within the context of the larger cultural scripts that don't recognize or acknowledge what it means to be a disposable and powerless human being in the workplace." That's why Gallardo's work with clients doesn't just involve conversations in an office but "often consists of making phone calls to lawyers, doctors, hospitals, bringing families into sessions together to assist in their continued transition in response to the drastic changes that have impacted them." He insists that he is not functioning in a role most often associated with social workers but rather doing the work he believes we *all* need to do with clients from underserved, disadvantaged communities.

We are all certainly aware that issues related to social justice, oppression, marginalization, and advocacy are an integral part of our responsibility as professionals; even more than that, it is part of our moral compass to stand up for the oppressed and fight against perceived injustices, racism, homophobia, and other forms of prejudice. Conference programs we submit often require us to discuss how the content addresses issues of diversity or advocacy. Leaders in the field often give impassioned speeches, admonishing practitioners to become more proactive in standing up for the rights of the dispossessed.

Indeed, we see token efforts everywhere: Post something on social media. Wear a ribbon or bracelet that proclaims support for a cause. Volunteer for a day with the homeless. Yet what it means to truly put our authentic selves into action involves far more than talk and token efforts but rather sustained commitment over time, far beyond what can possibly take place during a conversation in counseling. In a previous project, Jon Carlson and I collected more than two dozen stories from professionals who already had major work commitments in their teaching, counseling, writing, and supervision, plus family responsibilities, yet still found (or created) the time to launch advocacy and social justice projects and continued to support them over many years. What is the secret behind such an effort? It would appear that what makes any of us exceptional is not just our talk but our action.

Exceptional Counselors: Who *Are* They . . . and How Do I Become One?

Throughout this book, I have explored some secrets and ideas from the perspectives of a number of different practitioners and researchers. In addition, I have mentioned how during the past decade Jon Carlson and I were privileged to interview more than 100 of the most prominent theorists, scholars, and practitioners to ask them about what they believed distinguishes so-called master practitioners. Here is a summary of what we discovered as some of their most valuable secrets.

First of All, What Doesn't Matter Much at All

Most of the customary ways in which we might assign the label of *expert* to a counselor actually don't seem to count for very much. In the literature and research on expertise and mastery, within both counseling as well as other professions, theoretical orientation doesn't seem to matter, nor does your identified profession as a counselor, psychologist, social worker, or family therapist. Likewise, your preferred interventions and strategies don't necessarily qualify for designation as exceptional because the best among us tend to be highly pragmatic and flexible, customizing what we do to the individual needs of any given client and context.

Years of experience is often cited as a measure of exceptionality, as if just because someone has practiced for a decade or longer necessarily means that they are pretty great. But as we well know, it isn't how long you've been doing something that determines how skilled you are but rather how committed you are to practicing those things that you need to improve. For example, truly exceptional athletes or musicians are known not only to put in hours of rehearsal and practice every day but also to focus primarily on those skills they most need to improve instead of those they are already familiar with and good at. So it isn't so much how long you've been doing this job that counts the most but rather how committed you are to growing and to improving what you have already learned.

Personal Qualities

This comes up again and again in research and interviews with notable counselors: Who you are is as important as what you do. There is a consensus regarding which attributes seem to make the most difference, many of which have already been described. Ultimately we are in the business of influencing people, persuading them to do difficult things that they may often wish to avoid. We sell ideas. We present alternative ways of conceptualizing and framing problems, sometimes in ways that are quite at odds with what people have previously believed. We convince people to stop doing things that are not in their best interests and introduce alternatives that we believe are far more likely to meet their needs.

In order to be exceptionally influential and inspiring, we must exhibit a certain amount of passion and be seen by others as powerful models, however that is manifested. It is interesting all the different ways it is possible to do so. Although we are certainly familiar with the ways in which the charisma and big personalities of famous figures in the field draw attention to them and their ideas, it is just as likely that counselors who are far more soft-spoken and understated in their voices have just as much impact in their own way. That's what is so unique about our profession, that so many varied styles and different ways of being can be equally effective. The key appears to be that each of us has developed a therapeutic presence that best matches our personality, interpersonal style, and way of being and it allows us to capitalize on such attributes as compassion, caring, humility, wisdom, and composure.

The primary question we have been exploring throughout this book is this: What is the secret to becoming a more exceptional counselor? The answer to this is certainly found in the kinds of actions we take and the things we do in sessions, including the following:

- Following a path of reflective curiosity to search for knowledge, wisdom, and even enlightenment through the committed search for meaning in daily life
- Negotiating collaborative relationships that are best suited to the client's preferences, needs, issues, context, and culture
- Helping clients to feel understood in terms of not just their presenting complaints but also the meaningful aspects of their lives and experiences
- Processing emotional arousal in a multitude of constructive ways that reduce flooding and lead to greater clarity
- Facilitating specific therapeutic tasks and activities that help clients to meet their desired goals

- Demonstrating a high level of innovative thinking and creative experimentation in such a way that it leads to safe and powerful breakthroughs
- Viewing so-called difficult clients and challenging cases as opportunities for greater collaboration with partners in the process rather than as annoying impasses
- Soliciting ongoing feedback from clients regarding what is working best and what is not much appreciated at all
- Making continual adjustments in what we do, and how we do it, in light of the input we receive as well as our own honest and clear assessments
- Identifying and acknowledging our mistakes and failures so as to improve future performance
- Courageously challenging and questioning our actions and behaviors so as to constantly improve our effectiveness in a wide range of circumstances
- Practicing resilience and forgiveness with regard to our lapses and imperfections so we can learn from errors and misjudgments
- Providing support to people in such a way that they feel honored and held by us during such critical and difficult times in their lives

Ultimately, exceptional counselors are distinguished not just by what they do in sessions but by the ways in which they demonstrate commitment to continually challenging themselves to become more masterful. This applies not only to their clinical skills but also to the ways in which they practice what they preach in their daily lives. I've long considered it my greatest burden, in addition to my most valuable gift and privilege, that I have had this amazing opportunity to continuously grow and learn from my teaching, counseling, and writing. So many of the clients I've seen, students I've taught, counselors I've supervised, or readers with whom I've communicated have taught me so much about how change takes place and the multitude of ways this can occur and endure over time. After all these years, I *still* can't get over how fortunate we are to have chosen a profession that not only allows this but encourages it!

APPENDIX

Some Challenging Questions for Aspiring Exceptional Counselors

For those students and practitioners who have a strong desire and commitment to move beyond mere competence and achieve a level of mastery in their work, now and in the future, here is a list of some of the most meaningful questions that may be worth considering, either individually or in small groups.

1. How can you find your own voice when your head and heart are so dominated by other influences?
2. How do you limit your options by the ways you define yourself as a counselor and person, including your theoretical orientation, specialties, and style?
3. What are some of the most cherished beliefs you hold dear but have been unwilling to challenge critically in light of new opportunities and experiences?
4. What are some examples of how you tend to blame your clients or other external factors outside of your control when sessions (or other things) don't proceed the way you prefer?
5. What are some standard practices of the profession that have always bothered you but you've never chosen to challenge?
6. How do you explain the fact that there are so many different approaches to counseling capitalizing on so many distinctly different variables (past vs. present, cognitive vs. affective, relational vs. content focused, expressive vs. conversational, insight vs. action), and yet all appear to be reasonably helpful and effective?
7. In what ways do you feel confused and uncertain about aspects of your work but don't feel safe or comfortable admitting this to yourself and others you trust?
8. How do you live with your doubts, imperfections, mistakes, and failures, treating these experiences as valuable gifts and learning opportunities?

9. What are some ways in which you use your work to hide from unresolved issues in your life or compromise your personal relationships?
10. If you are really, *really* honest with yourself, what are some of the biases, prejudices, and entrenched beliefs that lead you to judge others critically, inaccurately, or unfairly? These could be based on race, economic status, religion, ethnicity, age, sexual orientation, or gender or even involve personal appearance, profession, or another characteristic that consistently triggers negative reactions.
11. How have some of your clients been your greatest teachers? Think of a few clients in particular who taught you some incredibly valuable lessons about the nature of counseling or, just as likely, helped you to (inadvertently) look at important parts of your own functioning.
12. In what ways could you broaden or diversify your life through new experiences, exposure to different stimulation, immersion in novel cultures or environments, and exploration of new subject areas?
13. What are some things you are willing to commit yourself to that will invigorate your practice and instill greater passion in your life?
14. What proactive steps could you take to recruit new mentors who might inspire or support you to move to the next level of personal and professional mastery?
15. Who are some friends or colleagues with whom you could safely and honestly talk about these questions and look more deeply at those that feel most threatening or challenging?